Moods of the Ohio Moons

Moods of the Ohio Moons

AN OUTDOORSMAN'S ALMANAC

Merrill C. Gilfillan

THE KENT STATE UNIVERSITY PRESS
Kent, Ohio, and London, England

© 1991 by The Kent State University Press, Kent, Ohio 44242
All rights reserved
Library of Congress Catalog Card Number 90-46805
ISBN 0-87338-436-9 (cloth)
ISBN 0-87338-437-7 (pbk.)
Manufactured in the United States of America

Illustrations were designed by Alvin Staffan and originally appeared in the *Ohio Conservation Bulletin*, September 1964.

Library of Congress Cataloging-in-Publication Data

Gilfillan, Merrill C., 1910 –
    Moods of the Ohio moons : an outdoorsman's almanac / Merrill C.
Gilfillan.
        p.   cm.
    ISBN 0-87338-436-9 cloth (alk. paper) ∞ ISBN 0-87338-437-7 pbk. (alk. paper) ∞
    1. Natural history—Ohio—Outdoor books.   2. Seasons—Ohio.
I. Title.
    QH105.03G55   1991
    508.771—dc20   90-46805

British Library Cataloging-in-Publication Data are available.

*In loving memory
of my parents
Clarence and Bertha Gilfillan*

Contents

Moods of the Ohio Moons

Introduction

For almost thirty years I have written an outdoor column devoted primarily to describing and creating moods about the world of nature. These columns were informed by a rural background and more than sixty years of outdoor experience as contained in field notes made at the time. They tap undying memories. These twelve essays, one for each month, relate incidents and events that contributed heavily to the mood of the time. They are based on columns that appeared in the *Columbus Metro Parks News, Ohio Conservation Bulletin Mood of the Month, Wonderful World of Ohio Magazine Outdoor Ohio,* and *Columbus Dispatch* "It's the Season" as well as in *Country Living* magazine articles.

Observation is more of the mind than of vision; our attitude is the secret of original observation. I choose the subjective approach to outdoor enjoyment. I did this after training in zoology and doing twenty years of field work as a wildlife biologist. I first became aware of the great difference between the subjective and objective methods when I read Van Wyck Brooks's *New England: Indian Summer,* a literary history, wherein the author points out that poets are often more accurate in their observations of nature than scientists. Early American poets described a hemlock woods so well that the description endures 150 years later, whereas contemporary scientific descriptions have been revised many times and still cannot match the revelations of the poet. The differences were so profound that I began to notice and compare.

Another example leading me to subjective observation occurs in James Agee's *Let Us Now Praise Famous Men.* In the third

"On the Porch" sequence with which he ends the book, Agee relates an experience that he and the photographer Walker Evans shared while awaiting sleep on the front porch of an Alabama sharecropper's cabin. They heard an unknown night call, one that was repeated, then answered by a fellow creature. Agee's description of the unknown sound and of the dialogue between the two calling creatures, his discussion of it, and the nurturing of the theme much as a composer might have developed it are superb. They lend a dimension to the mysterious event (and thus to all existence) that mere identification could never have given and increase the enjoyment beyond reckoning. Agee's personal, subjective treatment of the event is what renders it distinctive.

The final proof of the value of subjective enjoyment came from reading Marcel Proust's *Remembrance of Things Past*. Proust would occasionally experience an unaccountable feeling of great happiness, ecstasy, certainty, release from his almost constant anxiety, and the purest joy he had ever known. He noted that this state was triggered by commonplace experiences. One day, for example, he ate a cookie dipped in herb tea and had the instant transport to this pleasant state. He was puzzled and haunted by the mystery, and he sought an answer to the riddle.

Other experiences that affected him similarly included stepping on an uneven cobblestone street in a strange city, hearing a certain musical phrase, observing the glow of eventide on a restaurant wall, opening a childhood book, seeing a row of tall trees on a distant skyline. There was no reasoned solution to account for this state, and he began to earnestly seek an answer to bring peace of mind and understanding to himself.

Eventually he found the answer. Individuals change constantly; reason is not equipped to deal with inner change resulting from the gradual accumulation of one's past. Only the sensual, the sense-receiving endowment, which remains the same throughout life, can recollect the past in a tranquil state. Some of these sensual impressions at times of great joy slip into the subconscious mind unperceived by the individual and thus are untainted by thought.

Recollection, free of association with the present, recalls completely the freshness of the actual moment of occurrence. During this magical spell of a return to the past, Proust actually lived in the hopeful atmosphere of that fertile time and had choices available to him then. He had stumbled onto a way to go home again, only the trip couldn't be willfully recalled. It occurred when, by chance, some sensual experience opened the door of the subconscious for a brief return to the past. This sensual recall is the only reality to an intelligent, imaginative person, Proust writes, for it is wholly and solely his, a completely individual experience. Many reject it until too late because it is their own and they undervalue themselves.

Such experience is the heart of individuality. Since it is not subject to willed recall, it is necessary to explore the subconscious level of understanding. There the answer may be found, and it is yours alone to find. Here is Proust's message for nature observers: In observing nature, he writes, we pay more attention to the object than to our impression of it, thus ignoring the really original aspect, our own "view" of it. In other words, we should learn to seek our own original view of what we observe. We should live in a manner that will stock our subconscious storehouse with an abundance of original sensual impressions, which may later surface in our consciousness. Thus we may find the reality (truth) that was intended for us from the beginning. Do not die before the truth intended for you—your own individuality—is revealed to you!

To me, this is convincing proof of the value of the subjective method. The scientific method is necessary to gain facts, but the manner in which one experiences the facts is what will determine their final value to the individual, and, perhaps, to society. It eventually occurred to me that from my experience I had personally discovered romanticism two hundred years after the movement had its first stirrings. Initially I didn't recognize it because of my strong personal involvement in pursuing the subjective approach, but the knowledge had grown out of my dedicated pursuit. It became apparent that each individual must experience the romantic movement for himself or herself. When the discovery comes as a result of strong personal involvement, the person is convinced much more so than if he or she had studied the movement and intellectually decided to follow it.

The elements of this method are simplicity, a reliance on spontaneous sensual and emotional reaction to experience for the most creative pleasure, and a return to nature, supplemented by imaginative interpretation. This results in a highly personal vision, one which may be mystical and often highly symbolic. The method lends force and vitality to the person and to the pursuit. Thus, the heart of romanticism—the subjective approach—gives man a sense of his energy and of his limitations. It is the purest realism, contrary to its critics, for it is entirely the individual's own. It enables him to identify fully with the world about him and to express what he experiences lyrically and often dramatically, coloring his observations with richness and variety. Balanced with a sound basic knowledge of the outdoors, it permits the individual to make creative growth, to move away from cold conformity. He becomes a more natural person.

The subjective approach has brought me great personal satisfaction and pleasure; it has resulted in a greater understanding and appreciation of nature. In the process, I became what I was originally intended to be when I switched from an objective, scientific attitude to a highly personal subjective one: I am much more natural and at ease following natural gifts than following a learned approach.

Each person should learn to read his or her own book. Contacts with Mother Nature are an excellent place to start. The enjoyment of the outdoors should be purely subjective for the greatest personal reward.

The order of the material in each essay is as follows: weather, diagnostic events, vegetation, birds, mammals, other wildlife, agriculture, the wild harvest, and finally, a summary of the mood of the month. There may be repetition from month to month because there is repetition in the events of nature. Each month has its mood established primarily by the cycles of nature and only secondarily by man. The Indian moon names are purely of the North American continent; they arose from living with nature rather than exploiting it.

The wild harvest is important simply because it comes from untended nature. Carl O. Sauer, a cultural geographer, writes of the evolution of agriculture in relation to the development of man, and he emphasizes the importance of the wild harvest to early man and its contribution to the development of farming. Sauer's strong feeling for this development helps to explain why so many have such a strong atavistic urge to participate in planting and harvesting, and in gathering the wild harvest.

I have included much on agriculture because of its importance to the landscape we view, and also because of my farm background, which greatly influenced my attitude toward the world of nature. Man's relation to the soil is strong because of this early contact with the earth. It accounts for the need to get back to nature. For this reason, all forms of outdoor activity are dealt with, the many forms of nature study and the various ways of the ancient harvest: hunting, trapping, fishing, and gathering wild plant products—potherbs, roots, fruits, and nuts. Modern man has such great need to reestablish relations with the earth that any form of enjoying the outdoors is extremely valuable to society; all should be encouraged.

Phenology and the sense of seasonal progression are of constant concern since they contribute so greatly to the mood of any given time. Old sayings and folklore are also included as an important part of the mood process. Finally, the trends of land use and wildlife populations are mentioned because they are interrelated and so striking to the observer.

One of the most intriguing aspects of nature study involves time. Time has been defined as the sequential arrangement of events or as the interval between events. This arrangement gives a sense of progress, order, and change to existence. Time and space cannot be separated. Our experiences in space are meaningless without a sense of time.

Time is an unending flow, one with which we change. But, if a person constantly changes, what endures? Memory! The present is meaningless without reference to the past and anticipation of the future. Human life might be defined as the consciousness of time. Therefore, time is highly personal, and the subjective attitude is extremely crucial for human identity.

Since subjectivity is the reality of time, one's attitude and awareness cause it to go fast or slow, or cause one person to be keenly aware of its passing and another to be unconscious of its flux. Time flows continuously, and our sense of it is colored by association. Dynamic, unique events are milestones in our memory.

The inner world of experience and memory exhibits a structure causally determined by significant subjective associations rather than by objective connections to which we usually attribute it. Values and emotion strongly color memory and influence our sense of time. The serial order of time may be changed by memory. Time is meaningful only within the context of personal experience; it thus becomes qualitative whereas scientific, measured time is purely quantitative.

Memory is the self; it is creative imagination. In memory, the quality of an experience is preserved in its original state; there it attains an eternal essence and becomes more real, in a sense, than the original event. Memory research, as it might be called, can turn up rich and unsuspected facets of one's self and one's world, and outdoor study can amplify such efforts. Indian moon names illustrate the relationship between nature and the seasons. The Indians, entirely dependent on nature, had ample time to observe, and important events lodged in their memory, coloring it by dynamic association. Hence, their subjective moon names capture an eternal essence of the time, revealing far more about the period than the European names for the months.

In the time of primitive man, regular occurrence of the changing phases of the moon was one of the most readily observable events in their world, and it became the most logical means of dividing time. It was a short step from using the cycle of the moon as a unit of time to using names to distinguish one moon from another, and the moon names that evolved were rich in meaning. The names grew from conditions and characteristics of the particular moon period, such as changes or beauty or danger, and these conditions led to hope, joy, fear, or dread—attitudes expressed with wistfulness, gentleness, or harshness. They served as reminders from one generation to another of the important events for the tribe during particular moon phases. Moon names thus tell much about the people who devised them and of the region in which they originated. The names reflect and preserve a sense of values.

I sincerely hope this book conveys to the reader the impact of the many dynamic wonders of nature.

January

January was the Cold Moon or the Snow Moon to American Indian tribes. The names were well justified, for January is truly the heart of winter. During this austere month, there is commonly solid winter from Lake Erie to the Ohio River. The lowest average temperatures and the deepest snows usually occur during Quaker First Month.

January blizzards will frequently isolate an area. Anyone who has ever been snowbound has discovered the joys of isolation once the initial shock and fear are over. It is what Emerson described as "the tumultuous privacy of storm." Rarely in this world of haste and social compulsion does an individual have the opportunity to break fixed habit patterns and return to the old, natural rhythm of self—the true self. Being snowbound is one way to do this. Then, old buried attitudes return, and once again the person is natural and productive. Thought patterns are basic and original, decisions easy and right. Man-made plans mean little; nature calls the tune to which we dance for a time.

This return to true selfhood is important. It is essential that it be triggered while an individual can still return, before he is no longer able to do so, to what was really intended for him by nature. It is a matter of being reborn again to what he actually is—his whole self.

When snowbound, survival—meeting immediate needs—becomes the important factor. Merely making the best of the present situation becomes imperative; keeping warm, well-fed, and out of danger is the goal. Rural families develop a special mood of helpfulness and thoughtfulness; they give livestock an

7

extra measure of feed, perhaps a token of thanks that they themselves are less subject to the elements than their beasts.

Families learn to welcome freedom from routines imposed in
the name of progress and a higher standard of living. There is
time for leisurely meals, reading, writing letters, contemplation
in a renewed state of mind. Above all, there is time to notice and
appreciate the individuality of those with whom you live. If you
are caught short of supplies, you learn to appreciate the simple
fare that is available. While radio and television have taken away
much of the earlier sense of total isolation, the fact that travel is
impossible does impose a different point of view. Improvising by
necessity can lend a completely new sense of competence to the
man who relies on machinery to do once-manual skills. For the
first time in years, he may realize the sense of accomplishment a
pile of wood he has cut gives to him and to his dependents. He
knows the pleasure of being able to satisfy all needs in this simple rather than technological context.

A severe snowstorm brings not only isolation; it changes the
appearance of the landscape until new viewpoints are formed and
new relationships can be observed. During this unusual period, it
is easy to do fresh thinking with old landmarks and guideposts
out of sight or in unsuspected perspective. A snowstorm is only
one way of attaining this original selfhood, but it is the one most
likely to occur in January.

During this harsh month, wind is a dominant feature. Then
the cold breath of Boreas, god of the north wind, punishes the
earth's creatures. These cold winds can be cruel, but once safely
away from their force, the sounds are soothing. Wind has been
called earth's oldest voice, a voice of a thousand tongues, each
with its own mood. There is a softness in its rustling of fallen
leaves; it roars through barren winter woods and creates weird,
spine-tingling, banshee noises when branches rub together from
its force. It prunes dead branches and blows down dead trees,
disturbing woodland peace and perhaps causing a sleeping raccoon to open an apprehensive eye. Rarely winds find a chance
aeolian device, a wind harp, on which they play a variety of
pleasing sounds. When one is comfortably out of the wind, such
sounds stir the mind to pensiveness. I recall sitting in a country
schoolroom on windy winter days, almost lulled to sleep by the

mesmeric aeolian tones which varied with the force of the wind, a pleasant accompaniment to the timeless, peaceful setting. But when the boreal winds of January blow with blizzard force, wild creatures are at the mercy of the storm, and only good, dense cover and adequate food will keep them alive. Then marsh and swamp cover prove their worth to wildlife.

In early Ohio, the freeze-up, which we dread today because of exorbitant fuel bills, was welcomed. It meant relief from impassable mud, which sapped the energy of every creature that struggled through it. Heavy, clinging mud was an enemy! The freeze meant the beginning of relatively easy travel over the frozen surface of land and water. Visiting was done, and work neglected because of the mire was finally completed during the freeze-up.

But despite January's severity, warm spells do occur often enough that the term "January thaw" is a permanent part of the Buckeye lexicon. During these warm, foggy spells, coon hounds bay on hot trails—a sound of pure romance—as coons run, earthworms come to the surface, and tobacco comes "in case."

January is the Moon of Paired Tracks. Foxes begin to run nose to shoulder then, and the paired tracks tell that mating time is approaching. One January morning as dawn was breaking, I walked across a golf course to check a few traps. Suddenly, against the lightening horizon, I saw movement and stopped: It soon materialized into a pair of red foxes running and swerving in small, playful circles, much as two frisky, playful dogs romp with exaggerated movements, only with considerably more grace and delicacy. The male pursued the female in this frolicsome game, silhouetted against the light sky of the horizon in one of the most remarkable scenes of nature I have ever witnessed. The foxes either were unaware of my presence or they were so overcome by amorous impulse that they ignored me. The sight of this intimate scene of two extremely sensitive, cautious mammals' private love life was overwhelming. The intimate tag game continued until they disappeared over a distant rise.

Other mammals initiate their amorous rounds at this time, so paired tracks become a common sight in the January outdoors. At the same time, white-tailed buck deer lose their antlers; their mating season is over.

Because of the snow, January is a fine time to use or develop tracking skills. Ernest Thompson Seton, great North American naturalist, urged outdoorsmen to learn mammal habits by tracking: "Never forget the trail, look ever to the track in the snow; it is the priceless, unimpeachable record of the creature's life and thought, in the oldest writing on earth." This glowing statement emphasizes the pleasure and value to be derived from tracking; it can serve as the basis for sound life history information.

Squirrels are active all winter, searching for food they buried. Saucy red squirrels are especially active, and they track up an entire woods with their audacious antics. Following fox or mink tracks in the snow will prove to be an education in the maker's life history. Rabbits, too, track up the snow, especially on moonlight nights. The hibernators, notably woodchucks, are a comfortable five feet below the snow.

Most abundant of all the tracks are those of mice and other small mammals. Mice form the food base for many predacious mammals and birds and thus are invaluable to the larger forms. When mouse tracks are plentiful, there will usually be plenty of other tracks associated with them. The observant tracker is amazed at the large amount of wildlife that survives hunting and the knife winds of winter.

January was also known as the Wolf Moon, acknowledgment of the presence of hungry wolves near Indian camps. It is a lean month for wildlife, mammal, and bird, and winter hikers should carry feed for distribution along brushy fencerows and in other good cover where wildlife winters. Ear corn is nutritious and easy to carry.

On blizzard nights when man and beast seek shelter, one may hear, as I once did, the call of a great horned owl. I was returning home during a blizzard through deep, drifting snow. Finally, after many detours, I found an open route and arrived safely in the middle of the night. I crawled into bed, thankful to be warm when, above the storm's savage roar, I heard the insistent notes of a great horned owl. This call of the wild, more powerful than the storm's howl, brought a great sense of reassurance; there was still order and purpose in the world of nature. It made the blizzard seem less fearful, and I went to sleep strangely comforted. Not even nature's worst weather could stop this courageous creature from its appointed rounds.

During this month, it is the "staying" birds that nature lovers rely on for entertainment. Yard feeders attract many birds and provide endless pleasure to bird-watchers. Woodpeckers' staccato drumroll travels on the winter air; echoes of their industrious carpentry ring through the woods—an energetic, cheerful sound. Occasionally robins may stray into towns from the large flocks wintering in the wild grapevined hills. Cock cardinals flash brightly against the snowy background. On warm, bright days, their calls are louder and more ebullient. Tree sparrows' tinkling music is heard from weed patches. A marsh hawk flies low over some winter fields. Mockingbirds fly among the wild apple trees on a hillside, attracted there by the large apple crop that persists on the bare trees. Occasionally snowy owls invade the state. Along Lake Erie, the sight of a trim white owl perched on an ice jam is a highly prized experience. Hardy black ducks and mallards are frequently seen gathering gravel on creek riffles. Ruffed grouse drum, and the sound lures hunters to the woodlands. In a light snow, look for grouse tracks; the snowshoes they grow every winter show up well.

Few individuals are out on cold, moonlit nights, but such trips are rewarding. Many years ago on such a night when the thermometer was below zero, I helped the late Frank Hart set a net near Plain City to capture Hungarian partridges, which he was studying. We stretched the net, extending it from the top of a woven wire fence upward for three feet. Frank had observed that when the birds were flushed, they would soar over the fence, just clearing it. We worked for two or three hours in that unforgettably beautiful night, then retired to the local hotel with a great sense of accomplishment. Within a few years, Frank died in a train-auto collision in Plain City, but the memory of that night will last forever.

If the month is cold, ice fishing shanties will dot Lake Erie. Entire shanty villages will flourish as long as the ice is sound, and real fellowship develops among the ice anglers.

By January, most vegetation has deteriorated due to the weather; sleet and wet, heavy snows beat it down until it provides little protection for wildlife. Only in the wet lowlands does good cover persist. Cattails, for example, bend with and

deflect wind and weather upward and away from wildlife sheltering there.

Deciduous woodlands wear the rose-gray cast of winter. Hemlocks are Canadian life zone evergreens that occur in northeastern Ohio and in microclimates elsewhere in the state. They lend
character to a winter woods; their dark, pointed fir profiles are a
familiar sight to experienced outdoorsmen. Hemlock stands provide nesting habitat to some northern bird species not found
elsewhere in Ohio. Hemlock thickets offer protection against
winter cold, and winter feeding is often done there as well as in
marshes and swamps.

Noticeable plants in January include partridgeberry, where
grouse tracks are sometimes seen, and wintergreen, another favored grouse food. In sheltered, boggy sites, skunk cabbage will
occasionally peep through the muck. And in southern Ohio, the
first sugar maple trees will be tapped. Over most of Ohio the
heavy work of planting and harvesting is long past. Winter is a
period of rest, although there is wood to be cut, butchering to be
done and, when the ground is frozen, manure to be hauled.
However, in the cigar leaf tobacco country of western and southwestern Ohio, tobacco commands the attention, and there is
plenty to do. Tobacco, which was cut and hung in the shed to dry
in late September and early October, is not dry until late December. Usually during the Christmas holidays, when a warm foggy
spell arrives, tobacco farmers go into action. The damp air softens the leaves so they may be handled without tearing or shat-
tering; in this state tobacco is said to be "in case." The farmer
will feel the leaves repeatedly, testing them for moisture, and he
will sweep the barn floor clean and gather old tobacco bed covers
and other cloth.

After supper, the family goes to the barn to take down tobacco. The loaded tobacco laths are skillfully thrown to the floor
to land flat; then they are stacked in a square pile to a height
of six or seven feet. When all the tobacco is down and stacked,
it is covered with cloth; often shredded fodder is added to further insulate the damp tobacco from the cold and drying wind.
Frequently the work lasts most of the night. Boys chafe that
they are working on so promising a night while coons are
running.

January used to be a time for storytelling in this region. As tobacco was stripped (the cured leaves removed from the stalks), a warm fire flickered at the strippers' backs, and the job proceeded routinely enough that stripshed stories were inevitable. They usually dealt with past conditions in the community—uncleared land, inaccessible large swamps (by then cleared and growing corn), big timber, abundant wildlife, new ground farming, and the old country arts and skills (which weren't too old at the time). Many folktales and local legends had their origin in community stripsheds. The values of a community were never stated in a more elemental form than during tobacco stripping, for a discussion of religion was a standard topic, usually ending in a justification of local customs and beliefs. For me, stripshed stories and their lore are the essence of January.

I recall with nostalgic fondness the energetic preparations for blizzards in my rural youth. Large amounts of wood were stored on the back porch, livestock was doubly bedded, and an extra measure of grain was provided to help them endure the cold. Pumps vulnerable to freezing were wrapped with sacks, and every building was closed tight against the storms. In the frosty-windowed brick house, stoves glowed. Irons were heated, wrapped in thick papers and cloth, and placed in beds for warmth. Often we read around the fire later than usual. There was a large pan of popcorn and a dish of apples from the scent-rich cellar, and the comfort of the Moore's Three-Way heating stove. At bedtime we would undress around the fire and make a dash to the frigid bedrooms where the heated irons helped soothe the initial shock of cold bed covers.

Once in bed, the fierce notes of winter came to us uninterrupted. Strong, gusty winds howled and whistled and buffeted the brick house, making us fully aware of the threat of the storm. One of the last things I can remember hearing on such nights was Mother's prayer of thankfulness for our protection from the blizzard, and for help for those unfortunates, man or beast, who might be suffering from it. The security of that smoke-flavored past is endlessly comforting.

But for those who are active and daring, there are two kinds of richly rewarding hiking that can be done in January. For a rare treat, hike in a snowstorm; you will be privileged to observe intimate, peaceful scenes. Under such circumstances, I recall watching a flock of wary black ducks settling into a Portage County buttonbush swamp when dense snowfall limited visibility to thirty feet. Another time I saw a rabbit creating a new nest form in a leaf-banked briar clump during a snowstorm. I once heard a flock of Canada geese calling close overhead as they trafficked aimlessly, out of sight in the heavy snowfall, seeking an unseen little Ashtabula County lake. I witnessed from a woods a hunting fox jumping high above standing timothy, a bright red flash against the lonesome, snowy backdrop, as he sought to locate his fleeing prey. Again I watched a single file of white-tailed deer, dim figures confidently walking through the brush in the snow gloom. All of these creatures were behaving in a completely natural manner under the sheltering storm, unaware of my presence. It is a time of complete naturalness on the part of wildlife, and a special opportunity to the earnest student of nature.

Hike on a cold, snowy, moonlit night when the snow "zeeps" underfoot at every step. Listen for the great horned owl's low declaratory notes, soft even close at hand, yet with great carrying power like the low notes of an organ. The owls are staking out nesting territory in January, perhaps even nesting, and they may be called in at this time by a skilled hooter. The Sam Wharram Nature Club of Ashtabula County held owl hooting field trips every winter at which time great horned and barred owls were called in to fly overhead, snapping their beaks at the invaders.

Hikers may observe a rabbit dance if they are fortunate and quiet. This dance is a ritual game performed playfully and for reasons known only to rabbits. The quiet observer may see a few rabbits feeding or resting on the snow, when suddenly many rabbits will appear, beginning to run, jump, and twist in midair in a close, yet random formation. This feverish activity may continue for several minutes, then suddenly it stops and the rabbits fade into the snowy background. It is a mystic ritual, perhaps akin to the howling of dogs on moonlit nights.

These epic, intimate occurrences of nature lend a grand dimension to the night; they create a strange and wondering mood in the observer. While in this mood, scan the heavens. Observe the starry figures. Names of the constellations are rich in legend and mythology, and they ring with a sense of eternity that both stimulates and soothes the imagination. Probably Ursa Minor, the Little Bear or Little Dipper, is the most widely-known constellation because it contains Polaris, the North Star. Most individuals have sought the North Star to get their bearings on starlit nights. Ursa Major, the Great Bear or Big Dipper, is also well known. The Pleiades (the Seven Sisters) and Orion (the Hunter) are other familiar constellations, but there are a multitude to be found and their legends learned. After such invigorating trips afield, the fireplace is always more welcome.

To keep alive the precious memories of January, review the field notes of past Januarys. Such records are invaluable; they help to intensify appreciation of mid-winter nature. To record your experiences in writing makes them a more permanent part of you. And they help the observer to savor the mysteries he or she has been privileged to witness, perhaps eventually to share them with others.

February

February, the second month of the year by modern reckoning, was named for Februarius, an ancient feast of purification held in preparation for the new natural year, which then logically began with March. Our month of February starts with Groundhog Day on the second, a cheery bit of folkloristic hope that speaks of our longing for spring. It is an old European tradition that was changed somewhat in the transfer to America; our groundhog replaced the European badger in the switch. In pioneer America, the day served to brighten dull winter days in dark frontier cabins, hence its popularity and survival. The groundhog may sleep through Groundhog Day but human hope never does. The day is one way of bolstering the belief that seasonal order will prevail, that warmth and light will return.

February weather gradually gets warmer, days lengthen to equal those of October, and the month slowly becomes softer than January, even though storms do occur. February has been described as a capricious month during which warring weather systems strive for dominance. But hope for spring prevails, and spring sign becomes increasingly common. Winter is half over as February begins. There is an old country rule that if the haymow is half full on February 1 and if half the woodpile remains, both hay and fuel will last through to green grass and warm weather.

By the end of the month, the worst of winter is usually past. Then it is time for a cup of sassafras tea, the first Buckeye rite of spring. Sassafras tea has been renowned as a spring tonic for generations; among other benefits, it is supposed to thin the blood and get the user ready for hot weather, and it was drunk during Lent for this purpose. In colonial times, sassafras root bark from America was in great demand in Europe where it sold for a fancy price.

In the southern Ohio hills, the anxious residents dig juice-heavy sassafras root bark with which to celebrate the coming season. They dig and cut off a few large roots from a large tree, then fill the hole to protect the tree. The roots are scraped clean of dirt, the rough outer bark is rossed (removed), and the sweet inner bark is sliced off. This fresh bark, before it dries, makes especially delicious tea; it is the prized red bark the natives speak of. One ounce of root bark will make forty to fifty cups of sassafras tea if the bark is repeatedly boiled. When dug in early spring before the sap rises, it is strong and well flavored. It was once popular to boil the freshly dug root bark in maple sap; this produced an exceptionally delightful beverage. Now it is consumed the year round, hot or iced, usually sweetened with honey or maple syrup.

February was the Hunger Moon of the American Indians, a time feared by a people almost entirely dependent upon nature. It was also called the Moon of the Hungry Fox, a period when even this clever, resourceful being goes hungry. Even though the month's weather is an improvement over that of January, the effects of late winter are visibly hard on wildlife. Food and cover are daily becoming more scarce for the wild creatures. Weather has destroyed much cover at a time when it is most needed, so it is an excellent time to evaluate various habitats. Winter kills all resident creatures in excess of what the habitat will support.

The late Dr. Lawrence E. Hicks, first leader of The Ohio State University Wildlife Research Unit, always referred to marshes and swamps as the cradles of wildlife. Wetlands are more important to wildlife than any other single type of cover, he claimed, for they carry birds and mammals through the most critical period of the year. A lifetime of outdoor experience has taught me the solid truth of this claim.

Marshes and swamps are effective cover because of the dense, low level vegetation. They provide breeding and rearing sites, feeding and roosting cover, and escape from predators and harsh weather. In winter, wildlife crowds into these areas. Rabbits, bobwhite quail, ring-necked pheasants, and ruffed grouse seek food and shelter there. Deer escape hunters and free-ranging dogs by hiding in the dense wetland cover. Muskrats and minks build dens, and other furbearers—coons, foxes, opossums, weasels, and skunks—come seeking food and temporary shelter. Songbirds and small mammals also take advantage of the excellent cover.

But even while wildlife suffers the stresses of February's weather, amorous male skunks make their waddling black and white way across the winter scene, traveling in search of females. They may leave their wandering trails in the snow, the footprints tangential to the direction of travel, going from den to den in search of romance. From this early action will result another generation of pungency. It is a hopeful sign of spring, one that led some Indian tribes to call February the Skunk Moon.

It was also known as the Raccoon Moon by the Sioux, for coons also mate in February; their amorous squalling undoubtedly led to the name. Beavers pair off for the year, and the mating season of foxes continues well into February. In fact, the distinctive behavior of the mating mammals distinguishes the month.

Fox squirrels are often visible high in maple trees, nipping buds and twigs and licking the sweet sugar-sap; perhaps this is their spring tonic ritual, the equivalent of drinking sassafras tea. Red squirrels continue to track up the woods. Flying squirrels and deer mice make their homes in old woodpecker holes and other tree cavities; rap on such trees and you may frighten the occupants out to timidly stare at you. Chipmunks become active during warm spells, and groundhogs often clean their dens. During these spells, wildlife moves, causing a rise in accidental road kill.

The staying birds haunt the feeders and provide much of the early month entertainment. But those who do winter feeding should also do it in the wild, remote places, not just by the window. When I was working in the field as a wildlife biologist, I judged the zeal of cooperators by the amount of energy they expended in their cold weather feeding practices; proper winter feeding is difficult work. Carry feed to wildlife for their convenience and safety, not yours. This activity keeps the public involved; those who participate feel essential to the cause, a factor important to conservation success.

In the February woodlands, the squirrel-like churring notes of the red-bellied woodpecker are common. Hikers are often followed by chickadees and tufted titmice, the intimate birds of winter. The calls of cardinals grow throatier as the month progresses; in fact, most birdcalls take on the ebullient cadence of spring as days lengthen. Maple sugar house operators in lonely woodlots may see the first phoebe of the year when the newly arrived bird inspects the sugar house eaves, the site of last year's nest. Phoebes appear to be less abundant than they were fifty years ago. I suspect it is due to changes in bridge architecture as small rural bridges, always favored nesting sites, are replaced.

A pair of red-tailed hawks flies screaming through the woods, busy with early nest site selection. Along wooded streams, turkey vultures return "when lambing begins," according to an old country saying. Crows begin to ride the wind in smart alecky displays preliminary to March pairing. Great horned owls are already nesting. Sam Wharram, the diminutive Ashtabula County farmhand and an expert naturalist, used to startle his farmer friends on a cold February day by stating that he was going to the woods to look for bird eggs. They were even more startled when Sam returned telling them he had found what he went to find—great horned owl eggs. Barred owls are ready to nest now. Old time outdoorsmen had a saying that "every mountain is a better mountain for the bobcat on it." It would be equally true to say that every woods is a better woods for the owl in it. February is a good time to search evergreen thickets for regurgitated owl pellets. They are certain evidence of the presence of the night birds.

I recall visiting the Pymatuning Lake causeway every winter to see snow buntings that wintered there, feeding on weed seeds between the rocks with which the causeway slopes were riprapped. Sometimes there were ducks present; some waterfowl return in February if there is open water. Black ducks and mallards often winter on the ice near open holes, flying out to get gravel on the creek riffles. Winter kestrels are highly visible as they perch on utility wires, waiting for prey to move in the cover they scan. Doves feed in cornfields where corn-picker waste provides them with abundant feed, enough to hold them through the winter months. Unfortunately, fall plowing covers much waste grain and cover, both so important to wintering wildlife. Killdeers utter their sharp, clear calls as they fly through the cold air.

Large blackbird flocks roost in pine plantations; when flushed from their icterine rendezvous, the powerful wash from the thousands of wings bends the trees almost to breaking. The blackbirds muster at a point away from the roost, then return in huge flocks, peeling off to descend in a large funnel into the trees. In flight, they commonly stratify by species, as the late Dr. L. E. Hicks noted, with the starlings on top and the large grackles on the bottom. In between are the red-winged blackbirds, cowbirds, and rusty blackbirds. One large flock near Columbus contained an estimated 250,000 birds, according to Hicks. These giant flocks visit the meadows, swarming over them as those behind fly over and beyond the flock to forage in the lead in a continuous rolling movement, so characteristic of the spring landscape.

In years of abundant wild grapes, large robin flocks winter in grapevine-filled valleys. Often, when the food supply is depleted, they scatter and show up in towns and villages. Bluebirds, which winter in protected lowlands, also appear. Each is regarded as harbingers of spring when in reality they have been present all winter. Nonetheless, they are still a sign of spring. On bright sunny days, pheasant cocks crow; their overnight roosting sites may be located in marshy areas by the droppings they leave.

During this wintry time, snowy owls often appear, stirring our imagination. Occasionally these white ghosts will be seen perched on a fence post or flying over the winter fields. The sight always suggests the snowy arctic wastes. Several years ago, a snowy owl perched on a downtown Cleveland building in the bright glare of city lights. The pigeons and starlings left immediately while humans gathered to stare. How many watchers pondered the contrast between the severe economy of the bird's homeland and the lavish waste of energy the owl was blinking at?

But the event that captures most attention in February is the return of woodcock from the Gulf states to start their delicate, beautiful, prenuptial flight song, even in blizzard weather. Only the alert or informed will witness this first rite of spring. It has been described as the finest example of hope for things unseen. Usually Wilson snipe, which return at the same time, will be heard making their haunting winnowing sound from the sky, a weird, unearthly sound created by the wind rushing through their wing feathers.

Searching for and finding the oriental architecture of bulbous skunk cabbage spathes in boggy sites is the big event in the plant world for February. It might be blooming in favored sites. If so, honeybees may be observed visiting the flowers on warm days. Like the woodcock ritual, this event, too, is evidence of faith in things yet unseen but certain to occur.

There is other evidence of the soft season's approach. Red maple buds swell noticeably. Willow twigs take on a brighter yellow, and the kinnikinnick blushes a rosier hue. Sap rise occurs, little suggesting the strength of the great chlorophyllic onslaught to come. The most apparent manifestation of this early surge is to be seen in the sugar maple woods where trees are tapped and sugar houses are wreathed in steam clouds, a woodcut scene of early Americana. Mosses and lichens are prominent in the woods if there is no snow. Spicebush buds swell in rich woodlands. Coltsfoot may bloom in favorable exposures.

To the Delaware, February was the Moon When Frogs First Croak. Amphibians do get noisy during warm spells—primarily the spring peepers, the little frogs with the St. Andrews crosses on their backs. Perhaps they sing in celebration of Lent and approaching Easter. Salamanders lay their eggs in rocky streams. Freshet creeks take on a richer, spermy scent, what we used to call the smell of spring. Mourning cloak butterflies are on the wing, and the first insects splatter on car windshields.

Of all the winter tasks on the farm of yesteryear, cutting wood was the most engrossing. It is the task frequently mentioned when older rural people reminisce. It was difficult work, but there were many rewards. Mostly old, dying, or broken trees were cut, but occasionally a good timber tree would be chosen, usually an ash because of the ease with which it could be worked up. When the direction of falling was decided, a notch was sawed and chopped out to aid in felling the tree where wanted. Then the sawing would begin. Trees were cut as low to the ground as possible; this meant the sawyers had to bend double to saw. When the tree started to fall, they would quickly remove the blade and jump out of the way, for often the tree kicked back when the top hit the ground.

Trimming the tree with an ax would then begin. Limbs were cut and piled out of the way of the sawing task. Sawing off stove-wood lengths of the tree was easy "stand-up" work compared to doubling up to saw the tree down. The blocks were split at once, for when dry, they are more difficult to handle. A skilled axman would back around the block at a walk, slabbing off wood as he moved, reducing a sizeable block to stove wood in less than a minute.

The freshly sawn wood was pleasantly scented, an appetite-arousing scent. Birds would be singing or feeding in neighboring trees, and occasionally a rabbit would be seen backed up against a tree. The shotgun always accompanied the woodcutters, and the rabbit would end up on the dinner table.

With suitable weather, winter plowing can be done. In cigar leaf tobacco country, tobacco is stripped, boxed, and ready to be shipped by month's end. Along the Ohio River, gardens are spaded and some early garden is planted on warm days. In the undomesticated realm, the wild harvest is light this month. There is winter cress for greens; spring runs yield watercress. Ruffed grouse may be hunted through February, providing top sport and excellent table fare.

During this moody time of warring weather, there is a wide difference in the weather of northern and southern Ohio. Lake Erie is commonly icebound with huge piles of jammed ice dominating the scene, while in Ohio River coves there may be shirt-sleeve and sunbonnet days with families on the front porch. Spirits of the winter weary are low, but hope keeps building that the earth's ancient rhythm will again prevail and spring will soon appear.

In a quieter, more rural past, neighbors would exchange food items and have long visits to freshen the currents of existence while waiting for spring. They would share a mess of freshly butchered pork or perhaps a can of tart applesauce made from Northern Spies, Rambos, Baldwins (to lend a reddish cast), and other favorite varieties from old, familiar, backyard apple trees. The applesauce was piquant and full-flavored, the taste savored and remembered. There was depth to these ritual relationships in less hurried days when there was time to observe and detect need in others. But the most trusted method of keeping hope alive was to drink sassafras tea to foster the illusion that it would hasten the arrival of spring. In February, wildlife seeks food; man, no longer reliant on the wild harvest for sustenance, seeks hope in age-old spring sign.

March

Wild, changeable March Merryweathers, the wind-rejoicing month, is here. Officially it is two-thirds winter, but the equinoctial gales are winds of change. While there may be blizzard weather in March, the trend is toward spring; it is the time of the vernal resurrection. March sets brooks to chattering a spring jingle. Equinoctial storms may bring rain and rushing streams; the flood will change channels. Change is everywhere in March.

At the time of the vernal equinox, when days and nights are of equal length, winds may be especially gusty; they tidy up the landscape and dry and freshen the winter-soggy land. Shallow-rooted trees are often blown down when water-soaked soils and strong winds occur simultaneously. This creates "cradle knolls," a folk term of northeastern Ohio for the resulting side-by-side depressions and knolls that so often contain uncommon plants. Third Month winds start the action that breaks up the ice and starts iceout, an epic, vigorous event in the world of nature. These boisterous winds whip washings dry and full of sweet, vernal freshness, stirring human sensibilities to alertness. Kites ride high in the March sky. Oddly, the wind is never mentioned in moon names by the observant Indians.

Gales have influenced man in many ways. They helped to determine his travel and settlement, and often the success of his planting. The strong, persistent, many-voiced wind was blowing when man arrived, and it has accompanied him through the centuries. It may escort him off the planet if nuclear madness persists.

24

But there is usually sunburn weather in March as well as welcome warm winds. Then spring fever's siren voice sounds loudly; the beguiling ancestral voice of the red gods calls insistently, and office, home, and schoolroom become confining. Sun and sap break dormancy in the Awakening Moon. Vegetation makes its first noticeable growth of the year, a key indicator of the season's progress, for plants are a more accurate index of the year's advance than animals. Some Indian tribes named March the Green Moon in recognition of the greening grass. Nature changes from organic latency to quickness. The bulbous oriental architecture of skunk cabbage spathes is now prominent in boggy sites. Swamps may be tinged with red maple bloom, and budding progresses swiftly. Alder catkins appear, pussy willows show, and the first spring wildflowers of the year bloom. Furry-stemmed hepaticas blossom in corsages of pink, lavender, white, and deepest blue. An elderly Ashtabula County woman left indelible memories when she told of first seeing blooming hepaticas as a child. She had been riding on a sap sled drawn by horses through the snowy woods on a chilly March day as the family gathered maple sap. Her description of the event makes the cold March weather seem less formidable, and hepaticas the badge of spring.

The first potherb greens of the year may be gathered from favorable, south-facing sites. The task must surely be a response to a strong atavistic urge. Undeniably, gathering greens brings a sense of well-being and contentment long before the potherbs are eaten. The act may involve memories of accompanying a mother on a green-gathering expedition on some distant, spring-fevered March day.

Wild greens provide some of the tastiest, tangiest food imaginable. After eating the bland salad and potherb greens from the market, the taste of peppery wild greens will startle the taste buds. And the only cost is the effort required to walk the fields and fencerows to find them.

The most popular wild green is undoubtedly the dandelion. When this plant is collected before it blooms and before hot weather has toughened the leaves, it has a delightful, slightly bitter taste. Experienced green gatherers state that only white-stemmed dandelions should be picked; those with red stems are less desirable. Knowledgeable housewives of the past would always add other greens to their pot of dandelions, plants such as narrow-leafed dock, nettles, watercress, chickweed, violet leaves, and a variety of other edible plants according to season and taste.

Gathering greens is a rewarding return to the past, the time-flavored past when there was leisure enough to savor even the plainest fare. Heed the Old Testament advice, "Better a dinner of herbs where love is."

With warmer temperatures, animals become more active and their sign more prominent. The sight of highway-killed wildlife invariably accompanies a warm spell. Bats appear to make their erratic flight. Foxes squall and clean their dens in preparation for the arrival of young. A common village sound on March nights is the caterwauling of mating house cats, a spine-tingling sound more suited to a tropical jungle. Flying squirrels visit sap buckets on maple trees to share the sweet sap, and occasionally one drowns in the liquid.

The well-known hibernators come alive in March about the time of the waterfowl migration. Actually there are five true hibernators: woodchuck, bat, bear, jumping mouse, and thirteen-striped spermophile. These mammals all undergo severe changes in metabolic rate and are completely inactive all winter. Then there are the five "light sleepers": chipmunk, raccoon, skunk, badger, and opossum. These creatures sleep through severe cold spells but awaken and become active during thaws. Most noticeable when they appear in March are the woodchuck, chipmunk, and bat; the others are more secretive or rare in the state.

In birdland, the vital signs of replenishment ring out as the early nesters display, pair, and establish nesting territories; calls grow more fervent as the month progresses. The aerial display of pairing crows becomes more conspicuous as they tower and dive, riding the fitful winds of March at the peak of this activity, covertly selecting nesting sites.

The waterfowl migration grows in volume as the ice line retreats northward. During this month, ducks are pairing and are more trusting than usual; thus bird-watchers are frequently able to view them at close range. They are fresh from the south and in bright breeding plumage. The males put on elaborate courting displays to present a colorful show.

One of the most spectacular events in Ohio is the pile-up of migratory tundra swans along Lake Erie. This usually occurs in mid-March. The swans fly from the Chesapeake Bay area en route to their northern nesting grounds; often they encounter icebound waters further north. Then they congregate in the big marshes along Lake Erie, feeding in the surrounding fields as they wait for the thaw line to advance northward. This is one of the most magnificent sights in Ohio. The sight of two hundred to three hundred large, graceful white swans at relatively close range is a rare privilege. The soft calling of the large flock adds to the grandeur of the occasion and creates an out-of-this-world atmosphere. This epic event is so popular that it led the Ohio Division of Wildlife to hold a Swan Sunday in mid-March when the swans are commonly present. Large numbers of nature lovers drive long distances to view this majestic spectacle.

Being familiar with the pleasant call of the tundra swan, I have often wondered what the legendary swan song sounded like. The dictionary lists it as a fable, but in reality it actually happens. A Columbus man of my acquaintance once shot a swan, and his description of the event is fascinating to hear. When he shot, the swan, fatally wounded, set its wings and glided to a distant landing where it collapsed. It was calling constantly as it glided, a chilling, plaintive series of notes of great beauty. The man, a hardened hunter, was deeply moved by the experience, and he related the story at every opportunity.

Even more spectacular because of their greater numbers and clamoring calls are the Canada goose flights. Ernest Thompson Seton wrote of an Indian confined to jail because of a conflict with the white man's values. The Indian endured the imprisonment through the winter, but when he heard the clamor of geese beating their way north to their wild cradleland and sounding urgent calls of freedom, the restraint of his confinement became more than he could bear, and he pined away and died. Such is the power of the emotional passage song of wild geese.

Meadowlarks sing their "spring is here" song. Song sparrows cheer streamside thickets with their hopeful song. Territorial red-winged blackbird males flash their brilliant scarlet epaulets. The robin's matutinal caroling becomes regular, a hymn to the morning sun. Tree swallows dip and swerve over cold swamp waters. Great blue herons prepare for nesting in established rookery sites; little green herons squawk along creeks. In southern Ohio, mockingbirds chant their mimicry by the hour. Brown thrashers mock in rhyming couplets; it echoes from thicket and hedgerow. Starling mimicry is often a key to uncommon area birds. In northeastern Ohio, I learned to judge upland plover and bobwhite quail abundance by listening to starling calls.

Game birds call with seasonal urgency in March, and game biologists count the calls to gain an index to the species' populations. Great horned owls have young in the nest, and providing for them poses a threat to other wildlife. More turkey vultures ride in on the strong March winds, returning to streamside woods where they muster before scattering to nest.

Suckers come to the riffles when the weather warms, and other fish spawn. Night crawlers obligingly emerge to provide fish bait. Boys make early trips to fish for goggle-eyes and butterbellies around creekside stumps while song sparrow serenade bolsters their spirits. The amphibian chorus starts during warm spells, a chorus that will soon reflect the heartbeat of the land through the warm season to frost. Turtles sun on rocks and logs; the next day they may bury themselves in the mud to escape a sudden blizzard.

In March, outside work usually begins on the farm. Much plowing will be done with suitable weather, and some oats ground will be disked and sown. In tobacco country, as soon as the old crop is stripped, boxed, and shipped, preparation for the new crop begins. Tobacco plant beds are spaded early. The giant steam engines, once a major source of power on farms, are now used solely for the purpose of steaming tobacco beds to kill weed seeds. A tight steam box is fitted over a section of the spaded plant bed, and the soil is tamped tightly around it to confine the vapor. The section is steamed for twenty minutes to kill the weed seeds, then the box is moved and the process repeated until all plant beds have been thoroughly purged. This task is unchanged from the way it was first practiced. The sight of a smoking steam engine on a windy March day is a scene out of the past. In the burley tobacco country of southern Ohio, large brush piles are burned on the bed sites, a substitution for steaming. Then the tobacco seeds are sown, and homemade white muslin covers are fitted onto the bed frames as protection against the cold. These clean white tobacco bed covers are a distinguishing feature of the area; they stand out brightly against the spring landscape.

In times past, the figure of a lonely plowman walking behind the plow, guiding his team, was a landmark image on the raw, cold, March landscape. Long-tailed grackles followed him in the furrow, gleaning grubs and earthworms at his heels. Now such a nostalgic scene is possible only in Amish country or perhaps in the southern hill counties. One sunny March day, I drove to the farm near Plymouth Marsh where Sam Wharram, the eighty-year-old Ashtabula County naturalist, worked as a farmhand. Sam, a bachelor, had worked as a farmhand throughout his long life, moving from farm to farm where he was needed. As I approached the farmstead, I saw Sam plowing with a walking plow in a roadside field. The aged man was so short that he had to reach up to grasp the machine's handles. As I slowed, he stopped the team and stood looking up at the sky. When I got out of the car, I saw that he was watching a flight of northbound tundra swans against the blue sky, rosy from the sunlight on their white plumage. The scene of that diminutive figure standing by the plow, gazing up at the swans, left an undying impression of the man and of the pursuit.

Maple sugar camps are operated through March, especially in northern Ohio. This is another farm task little changed through the years. There is an old saying that when pussy willows form, it is time to close the sugar house, for the sap will soon be getting buddy. It used to be a custom in northeastern Ohio to hold sugaring-off parties late in the sap season. Each guest would receive a small dish of maple syrup which he or she would stir until it turned to sugar. This rich confection would then be eaten. To counter the effect of too much sweetness, coffee, crackers, and sour pickles would be available for the overindulgent. March was appropriately called the Moon of Making Sugar by the Chippewa.

The noticeable difference in weather for northern and southern Ohio becomes even greater in March. In sunny Ohio River coves, shirt-sleeved men and sunbonneted women plant potatoes while Lake Erie is still a desolate, ice-strewn wasteland. A northeastern Ohio saying has it that spring never comes to that region until all the ice is out of Lake Erie at Buffalo.

Many dedicated, earth-loving persons have a spring-welcoming place, a familiar spot where the order of natural events has been learned and the progress of the season can be noted. At such special places, they relax and let spring come to them.

April

April showers bring the proverbial May flowers and summer bowers of greenery. April is a wet, soft, gentle month, the first full month of spring biologically and astronomically. Protracted warm April rains bring a rush of spring sign. But valuable as rain is to the earth, weather-conscious farmers watch the skies, then their fields, as they hurry to plow and fit the soil.

The sun is north of the equator and getting warmer. Warmth and water cause the song of the earth to gain in volume and make known its many voices. It's the rebirth of the land with its regular, strong, seasonal pulse; it's the start of the showy pageant of nature. The song of the earth gains strength, and by the month's end it is well established. We start getting ready for summer.

April is the Grass Moon of some Indian tribes. The grass grows fast in a strong chlorophyllic surge. The sap-rise of March becomes sap-rush in April. Vegetation grows, leafs, flowers, and casts the first slight shade of the year. There are also many flowers in Fourth Month, even though May has more. They succeed one another in a constantly changing color pattern on the woodland floor. Skunk cabbage is still blooming in wet spots. The furry-stemmed hepaticas still show their corsages of blue, lavender, pink, and white flowers, perhaps the brightest spot in the early April woods. Spring beauties cover the woods floor; in low areas violets lay a royal purple carpet for the walker. Coltsfoot shows up on bare soil.

Trout lilies, dutchman's breeches, squirrel corn, bloodroot, anemones or windflowers, crowsfoot, sweet williams, bellwort, Virginia bluebells, giant flowering trillium-covered slopes, cranesbill, and the glossy scabs of mayapple patches, and in deep, moist gullies wild ginger and jack-in-the-pulpit—all of these spring blossoms appear in their given time, joining with or replacing other species to brighten April's woodlands. Much pleasure and dimension can be added to flower study by exploring the meaning of the common names of the wildflowers. Quite often these folk names reveal much about plants and the attitudes toward them. Old names such as wake robin for a trillium, cranesbill for wild geranium, mandrake, wild lemon, or raccoon berry for mayapple, and red puccoon or Indian plant for bloodroot evoke a sense of timelessness in the thoughtful nature student.

How many generations or even centuries does it take for a folk name to be earned by a plant or animal? Viburnum dentatum is called arrowwood because the straight stems were used by Indians as arrow shafts. Use may determine the folk name, as with arrowwood, or there may be a fancied resemblance; wild geranium is called cranesbill because of the resemblance of the pistil to a crane's bill.

In the acid soils of eastern and southern Ohio, trailing arbutus blooms in April. It is a shy, unobtrusive plant, but one that is extremely rewarding to find. Here are notes I made while visiting a large patch of this exquisite flower in Ashtabula County:

> I found a large patch of trailing arbutus growing with partridgeberry. The delicate white and pink flowers, nestled with the shiny red partridgeberries, made a startlingly beautiful picture. They were growing on hummocky soil at the edge of a hemlock-yellow birch bog in the midst of a stand of reindeer moss. Briars, wild cherry, and wild apple were taking over the site which was covered with leaf mold. The hummocky soil was dotted with cradle knolls. The heavy, sweet fragrance reminded me of mock orange scent. The abundance of tiny flowers was partially hidden in the profusion of rough, raspy leaves, and the fragrance was detectable downwind far beyond what one would have expected. A patch of wintergreen, ten feet in diameter, grew close by, and skunk cabbage and cattails grew in the lower spots.

Set against the backdrop of the dark, gloomy appearing hemlock growth, it was an intriguing, mysterious sight. In the edge of the hemlocks, I found a pile of owl pellets and some identifying barred owl feathers. The reindeer moss was crisscrossed with small mammal runs, indicating that there was an ample food supply for the owls.

The five-acre stand of 30–40-foot hemlocks stood atop a high hill overlooking distant Lake Erie, and its jagged, pointed fir profile so darkly green even in bright sunshine presented a strange, unexpected picture. The presence of this exquisite, retiring plant in this severe natural economy brightened the scene and the day. It was the vision and the breadth of spring. Oddly, there were no blueberry bushes present and I would have expected to find them there.

The shrubs are blooming in April. Fencerows come to brightness with downy wild plum and lacey Juneberry blossoms. Dooryard flowering quinces bloom late in the month, and the hummingbirds arrive in time to visit the flowers. Woodlands are largely gray but greening. Late in the month, entire hillsides become magenta-tinted with redbud, and dogwood begins to whiten the woods. Wet woodlands are marked by blazing red maple flowers early in the month. It is fire-watch time in the state forests. Before the green growth becomes dominant, the dry leaves burn readily, and fire-watch planes patrol the forests. In the past, fire watchers scanned the horizon from fire towers for telltale smoke.

The swelling dynamics of April applies to birds as well as to plants. Young great horned owls grow tall and feathery in the nest. Soon they will be ready to accompany the parent birds on their first hunting flights. Barred owls are just hatching. The bird population increases daily throughout the month; each morning new songs are heard. At dawn and again at dusk, the primordial bird music sounds much as it must have sounded in Eden; this chorus grows as the month progresses and on into May.

April is the Wild Goose Moon of northern Indian tribes. Then Canada geese fly over, sending down their inspiring calls. Yet to the Plains Indians, April was the Egg Moon, the time when the large birds, mainly waterfowl, returned from the south to start nesting. They laid large eggs—valuable as food to the Indians, hungry after a cold, difficult winter. During the nesting season, loud, distinctive breeding calls are common, so the sight of noisy, protesting birds over an extensive marsh must have been exciting to the Indian egg gatherers.

Ducks congregate in small groups on beaver ponds, swamps, marshes, and creeks; some remain to nest. A feature of the wet month is the sight of large numbers of shorebirds in flooded fields and on mud flats around lakes and other wetlands. When flushed, the shrill, strongly accented, penetrating cries uttered as they wheel and maneuver in swift, precise formations is one of the most exhilarating sights and sounds of the season. Migrating loons appear on the larger lakes; occasionally their low, yodeling call may be heard, just a suggestion of their full-voiced calls on northern lakes. From swamps and marshes, the American bittern hiccups his unique thunderpumping call, summoning up visions of its unusual performance, comical to those who have seen it. The bird goes through an exaggerated body contortion to bring forth this distinctive sound, humping and arching the entire body in the pumping effort. Sadly, with the ever-increasing drainage, this sound is heard less and less, a loss to all who have ever walked the land in April. Marsh hawks are frequently observed perched on high ant hills at this season, particularly in the poorly drained sections of the state, and they may be observed doing their spectacular aerial somersaults during mating season.

Some bird students have evolved a phenology of bird arrival. The Baltimore oriole arrives when peach trees bloom; flowering quince blooms as hummingbirds arrive, and Cape May warblers appear when cherry trees bloom, to mention just a few examples. Phenology, which has many followers in Europe, is gaining attention in America. The science adds dimension to nature study by involving more than one discipline. Phenology is the relationship between climate and periodic biological phenomena. Usually plant life is the constant since it is the most reliable index to the season's progress, and animal behavior is measured in relation to plant progress and development.

Many birds nest in April. The matutinal caroling of robins is a characteristic sound in town and village; this cheerful early song serves as an alarm clock for many. Brown thrashers are early arrivals and soon start the mimic singing; they are perhaps the best of the mimics. Advance purple martin scouts arrive early in April. Large blackbird flocks roost in the marshes. Some of the more brightly colored birds show up late in the month—orioles, rose-breasted grosbeaks, scarlet tanagers, and wood thrushes.

In late April, as the migration builds up, birds moving through Ohio pile up on the Lake Erie shore, feeding to gain strength and waiting on a favorable wind before crossing the lake. A major hawk migration occurs at this time, but the larger, stronger hawks do not cross the lake; they fly around it, following the shoreline. It has been suggested that, as predators, they fly over land, where prey is always available. Hawk watchers concentrate at the Ottawa National Refuge east of Toledo during this period. They scan the sky systematically, using the quadrant method; each day accurate records of several thousand migrating broadwinged hawks are reported. The strategic location of Lake Erie is a major boon to Ohio bird-watchers.

Captain J. Paul Perkins, retired Great Lakes ore boat captain from Conneaut, maintained a group of potted evergreens aboard his ship during bird migration, and he has fascinating movies and stories of birds that came to the ship, and of their behavior while there. Some birds are undoubtedly lost while crossing the lake; Perkins observed that many came to the ship exhausted. Birds migrating across the lake were not harassed by hawks, but Perkins reported that gulls recognize their advantage over water and prey upon many birds, even those as large as great blue herons.

Mammals are not as obvious as the lively, loud birds in April. They are busy giving birth to and caring for their young. Muskrats travel when flooding occurs, and many are killed on the highways. Fox squirrels also move and appear as road kills. While hiking, I once found a large female possum dozing along the trail. Her pouch was full of tiny young. The pouch was tightly closed, but the tiny wigglers could be seen by slightly opening it. Woodchucks are evident everywhere; so are chipmunks. But for the time being, most attention is turned toward birds and wildflowers.

Amphibians start to tune up. Peepers, the woods pond pipers, create a deafening cacophony—the principal April noise unless the month is exceptionally warm. Late in the month, the trilling of toads begins. One of the most imaginative names for a lonely cabin that ever came to my attention was Toad Trill; the name suggests remoteness and quiet except for nature's sounds.

The farmer plowing his land must be the most common sight on the April landscape. Today giant tractors roar across the fields, pulling gang plows with several shares and turning over a strip of land many feet wide on each round. It is a noisy, industrial operation rather than a quiet, pastoral task as it was in the past, and the noise dominates the community. When plowing with horses, the only sounds to be heard were the creaking harness as the team pulled, and the soft tearing as the plow share cut through the root-matted sod. The plowman had ample opportunity to listen to the gutteral, scolding notes of the big grackles that followed him, gleaning grubs and earthworms from the furrow.

A major portion of fitting the fields for corn planting was done in April in preparation of May planting. Driving a team to disk or harrow the soil to fitness could be a dirty job if the soil was dry and dusty. But these jobs, too, were quiet; the only sound was the constant friction of harrow tooth or disk on soil. Much oats is sown in April, especially if the spring is late.

Young livestock livens the farm scene; gangly calves, frisky lambs, and awkward colts add life and action. Their presence emphasizes the newness of the season. On sunny days the chicken house is filled with high, happy hensong. Early gardens are planted to supply the kitchen. Later, the truck patch will be planted to supply vegetables for canning, freezing, or storing.

Fish provides most of the wild food of April. A large number of anglers and a multitude of hungry fish results in a big catch. Fish from cold water are firm and well flavored. Dyed-in-the-wool anglers eat all the fish they catch, as do all boy anglers; all kinds appear on the table and are appreciated by the dedicated outdoorsman.

April's warm rains stimulate the fish population; fish spawn and go on a feeding rampage. Thus the Fourth Month is one of the better angling months of the year. Here's some fishing phenology: When dandelion bloom is thick, largemouth bass move to shallow water and start hitting. When buckeyes bloom, smallmouth bass go on a hitting spree and are more easily taken. Anglers agree with Dr. Henshall's famous statement that "pound for pound and inch for inch, smallmouth bass are the fightingest fish alive." Incidentally, smallmouth bass and suckers school together near riffles in April; the bass are much more active than the suckers.

This month fish management workers strip egg-heavy muskies and northern pike of their spawn, fertilize it with sperm from the males, hatch the fry, and fill hatcheries to grow fish to replenish lakes and streams. The large predatory species, such as muskies, are stocked to help control populations of smaller fish, which otherwise outgrow their habitat and become stunted. But muskies do more than control populations of smaller fish. They have been so successfully stocked in Ohio waters that large numbers are caught each year by sport anglers. At the annual Ohio Division of Wildlife-sponsored Huskie Muskie dinner, more than one hundred anglers are honored for taking a muskie meeting minimum club size requirements, and as many as one thousand anglers are recognized for meeting honorable mention size requirements. The addition of muskies to Ohio's game fish has provided untold hours of recreation for Ohio anglers.

In the spirit of the season, boys fish the spermy April waters for anything that will bite, and their anticipation is high. Any boy who has ever fished on a spring day knows more about hope and high expectations than one who has never enjoyed this experience.

Carp flop in the marshes in April as they wallow around preparatory to spawning, and archery fishermen wade the marshes seeking them. Early spring anglers of any variety are privileged to see many intimate scenes of the wild at their unpretentious best; all appear sooner or later to be viewed by the quiet fisherman. The angler may watch coons come to the water's edge to fish, carefully washing their food; they may see and hear the woodcock's first prenuptial flight song of the evening; they may watch a tireless mink explore every crevice and cranny of a stream bank. There's more to fishing than fish.

In the past it was the housewife who walked the fields and followed fencerows to hunt potherb greens. They passed on their

wisdom in such matters to sons and daughters. But today most
green gatherers are men, outdoorsmen who have a strong provider instinct and a taste for the unique wild greens. They gather
the potherbs according to individual taste and training in the art.
Americans have been wasteful of the lavish supply of wild potherbs available for the taking. Europeans make much greater use
of them, perhaps a result of the crowded, more competitive living
conditions there. But we'll get there soon if present population
trends continue.

Cowslips or marsh marigolds are especially fine as greens.
Usually in April, cowslips grow to a usable stage in the wet sites
they occupy. They were so highly prized in New England that
they were gathered and offered for sale in the Boston markets at
a good price. If possible, they should be cut before they bloom. I
cut them low enough to include the thick, mucilaginous stalks as
well as the stems and leaves to add to the fine, rich flavor.

In West Virginia, ramps festivals are held each April at the
start of trout fishing season. Eating ramps is jokingly referred to
as a rite of initiation into manhood. Actually the onion-like bulb
is very tasty when parboiled; it is also excellent when pickled. In
the distant past, the bulbs and leaves were used to flavor soups
and other dishes. They must be dug before the leaves die down
or else they can't be found.

Spring fever usually hits during warm spells in April. Then
the lure of the open road is strong and the vagabonding spirit
surfaces. The theme song of this spring fever restlessness is well
expressed in an old school song, "Follow the road that beckons
with lazy grace as it loiters in the sun." The events of April
combine to lend a sense of promise of great adventure if one will
only follow the path to freedom.

April's ideal weather is much briefer than that of May, but no
less appreciated, and the high anticipation which the coming season generates adds to the charm of the idyllic spell. Easter often
falls in April, celebrating the renewal of the earth as well as the
promise of hope to many, and it adds to the sense of expectancy.
John Burroughs wrote of the "crystalline days of April, days of
warmth and clarity when the earth seemed new." April is the
start of natural abundance, an abundance which lasts until frost.

Bird migration is in progress and gaining strength, the powerful chlorophyllic thrust of plant life is growing stronger, and the warm weather hastens and strengthens both. Imagine the vast energy unleashed as millions of birds fly across the continent, and trillions of plants vigorously thrust upward.

There are many ways to capture the mood of this month: go fishing, watch for new bird arrivals each day, follow a spring run to hunt early spring sign, gather wild potherbs, or go vagabonding by following the lazy road that loiters in the sun. They will all lead you further into spring.

May

May is traditionally a happy, carefree time. New Englander James Russell Lowell's line, "What is so rare as a day in June" can be applied to much of May in Ohio. Usually the showers of April have subsided and the weather is near ideal. Yet none of the Indian moon names for May relate to the weather. A popular Indian pictograph for May shows a singing bird perched on the handle of an Indian planting stick, a combination of two moons, the Song Moon and the Planting Moon. Most Indian moon names reflect an absence of a sense of time, certainly of clock time. But they evince a strong sense of seasonal rhythm, sometimes happy, often appealingly sad.

May is the pleasant stretch from showery April to comfortable early summer. The month often starts with wet feet and ends with the more stable weather of June, usually considered summer in Ohio. Fifty years ago, when rural schools let out in late April, May was considered by children to be the beginning of summer, the start of endless days of idyllic, barefooted nothingness, of roaming the countryside with a passion born of the season itself. Its sweet breath restores beauty to the earth, advancing what was well started in April. During the Moon of Flowers, the dynamics of the organic urgency staggers the imagination. It is the Emerald Month to one who regards the wide expanse of bright green grass starred with dandelion gold. The statement of a man from a desert region on seeing Ohio when the grass was at its healthy, brightest best explains the wonder of abundant grass: "It grows everywhere, even right up to the buildings," the astonished man exclaimed. What great appreciation for a blessing we take for granted! Every plant forms the base of life for some creature. All flesh is truly grass, as we are told in the Bible. In May it might be well to think on the importance of this renewing growth to animal life. All that we value rests on photosynthesis, the process by which the earth's inorganic materials are converted into the foods all living things must have. Spend some time just admiring a grassy plot or luxuriant field of rich green clover. One farmer said that he never witnessed the sight without feeling an urge to drop on all fours to feed with the cattle. And in the midst of this bountiful realm of photosynthesis, we enjoy the quietude of natural events. Natural sound is not harsh when heard against the backdrop of an outdoor setting. Most of the sounds of nature are free of compulsion, pressure, and pretense.

May is a month for spectacular blossoms. Woods floors, carpeted with wildflowers, are as cheery as the most imaginative, brightly patterned carpet. Spring beauties and purple violets are the most common wildflowers. Bloodroot, sweet williams, bellwort, giant flowering trillium, patches of Virginia bluebells, mayapples, buttercups, anemones, and cranesbill fill the woods. Deep, moist gullies harbor wild ginger, jack-in-the-pulpit, and perhaps showy orchis. In southern Ohio, the state forest hills have orchids—pink moccasin flower and small yellow lady's-slipper—blooming.

Redbud is fading. Flowering dogwood blossoms, May's treat, are so well known that special trips to view them are popular. The lacey blossoms of Juneberry or shadbush (shad run in the rivers during its blooming) still brighten woods, and the maddening fragrance of wild crabapple flowers will perfume the downwind air for unbelievably long distances. Elderberries start to bloom late in the month; there is an old country saying to never cut down hay during the elder blossom rains. If this advice were adhered to, little hay would be made for elder blooms throughout the summer.

In northeastern Ohio, the tiny waxen bells of blueberry blossoms appear early in the month. When I ran woodcock census routes in this region, the blueberries were always blooming during the height of the woodcock singing ground ritual, a pleasant phenological association. May is a burgeoning month, with bright beauty on every hand!

The Wabanaki Indians properly called May the Song Moon. The matutinal and vesper singing of birds is one of the most esthetically stimulating events of the world of nature. This avian hymn to the sun is a sound out of freshest Eden. The morning song has been interpreted anthropomorphically as thanks for a safe night and for the appearance of the sun; the vesper song is given in thanks for a day of abundant insect food.

Birdsong from woodlots in farmland forms islands of ebullient sound and activity; the person approaching a woods does so with a certain amount of awe and wonder. I recall walking down our long Darke County lane after the cows early in the morning, listening to the powerful outpouring of birdsong, fascinated by the musical babble of hundreds of voices. I was drawn to the woods, mesmerized by the compelling, hopeful music. It remains one of the vivid impressions of youth.

The bird migration peaks with the arrival of the warblers, sometimes called the singing butterflies. May is warbler month to dedicated bird students. The birds arrive in Ohio about the time trees start to leaf, and birdwatchers experience anxiety as to whether the warblers will arrive before leaf-out; when the leaves expand the birds are difficult to find in the leafy trees. The warblers are the brightly colored wills-of-the-wisp that try the beginning birder's will.

The May migration includes some of the most brightly colored birds alive; they are brilliant without being gaudy. The flaming orange head and throat of the Blackburnian warbler, seen in early morning or late afternoon red sunlight, reveals the most stunning of Ohio birds. The satiny radiance of the scarlet tanager in the May sun is another color treat; the bright scarlet contrasts with the black wings and tail, rivaling the tropical birds. The fiery orange and black of the Northern Oriole flashing through spring foliage or perched in a blooming cherry tree adds another dimension to beauty. The rose-breasted grosbeak appears in formal dress—black jacket, white shirt, and a flowing rose-colored tie—and his robin-like caroling is a welcome sound. These birds add to the high sense of May madness.

   Some of the finest musicians arrive in May or are in full voice
then, and the woods are enriched by their songs. The wood
thrush dutifully flutes his delicate, ringing phrases; a heavily
spotted breast and rufous-red head add to his beauty. From the
wet swamp forests of northeastern Ohio, the wheezy, breezy,
Pan-like, waterpipe music of the veery comes, a downward spiraling, seductive song that will almost coax the listener into the
mosquito-infested woods. I recall the day I learned to associate
this wheezy call with the plain, unobtrusive bird that uttered it.
I chanced to be watching a veery through binoculars when it
sang the mysterious song I had so often heard, and the discovery
brought great elation. From deep gullies the rhythmic call of the
ovenbird rings, companion to showy orchis and wild ginger.
Blue-gray gnatcatchers whine in the tree tops. Birdcalls are so
insistent that it is often difficult to isolate one for detailed hearing. During this dynamic, noisy time, many birders try for a
century day, a day in which they observe one hundred species, a
magnificent accomplishment for most.
   Perhaps the birding I remember best was done in Ashtabula
County. This biologically rich area boasts of the largest number
of breeding birds of any Ohio county. It is northern in character,
lying in the transition life zone, and offers a wide variety of habitat types. The swamp forests, which have standing water in the
spring, harbor many species during migration. I would roam
these wet woods for long days, forgetting lunch as I sought to
identify the many species that were new to me, looking against
the bright sky until severe headache forced me from the woods.
Those swarming, flitting birds feeding above the large woods
pools possessed an addictive fascination, one which caused me to
endure an aching neck and eyestrain in trying to become ac-
quainted with them. To this day the memory of those bird-filled
swamp forests remains as one of the greatest, most enticing
scenes from outdoor Ohio ever etched on my memory.
   I recall many specific incidents involving birds through the
years. As a boy, I often found killdeer nests while harrowing
fields to corn-planting fitness. My father would insist that the
nest area be marked and an undisturbed island left to protect the
nest until it hatched. Frequently, movement on raw earth would

call attention to baby killdeers—bumblebees on stilts we named them. The weary, sweet, killdeer lament of late summer had to be paid for with such attention.

The flicker's courting display was always entertaining; the humorous bobbing, the spread wings and weird vocal effects attracted attention. The bubbling, ecstatic songs of bobolinks and meadowlarks flying over fragrant clover fields remains a portrait in purest pastoral romanticism.

I recall countless May days with deep pleasure, but one that often comes to mind occurred in Plymouth Marsh in Ashtabula County long before highway I-90 was located across its northern edge, detracting from its wild appeal. I had wandered through the marsh for three or four hours, observing many species of birds in this biologically rich wetland, when I heard a quavering sky note, "who-who-who-who-who," coming from high above. I listened and watched. Finally a bird form materialized, circling and swerving downward, all the time continuing to make the unearthly sound, a sound Thoreau so accurately described as "spirit-suggesting." The bird alighted on a fence post before me—a Wilson's snipe! I had heard the sound many times before but had never identified it. Suddenly, to my great contentment, the mystery was solved; the sound, I later read, is made by wind rushing through the snipe's wing feathers. It remains another of my most cherished memories of wide, wild places, of high-vaulted, blue May skies, and a natural event out of Eden. I had always referred to it as a cosmic song before I learned to know it, and still think of it in this context.

In May, some of the great songs of the earth are to be heard. Many years ago, I spent a May weekend walking the swamps and marshes of Michigan with Dr. Lawrence Walkinshaw, the sandhill crane authority, searching for nests of these magnificent birds. I was fortunate enough to find one. Usually the birds are described as gray, but those I saw were tinged with brown. The tall crane's stately tread and the slow bobbing of the red-marked head lent a noble appearance. When the crane was frightened from the nest, it let out the powerful, clarion call for which it is renowned, and the calling continued as it flew, a flying cross, circling and climbing until out of sight in the sky. Even when the bird was no longer visible, the compelling call still came down to us. All sounds of nature have charm and meaning to alert listeners, but there are some so stirring that they must rank among the epic songs of the planet. Such is the call of the sandhill crane and the musical clamor of a flock of tundra swans. They are among the inspiring sounds of the earth. On the same epic magnitude are the haunting passage song of a flight of Canada geese and the unearthly yodeling cry of the common loon.

Those who visit the wet areas of the state in spring will flush flocks of shore birds; the sight of these large flocks in flooded fields and on mud flats around lakes or swamps is distinctive. When flushed, the shrill, strongly accented, penetrating cries uttered as they wheel and maneuver in swift, precise formations are one of the most exhilarating sights and sounds of the season. If greater yellowlegs are in the flock, their cries will dominate the performance; their ringing, imperative three or four-noted calls and the fast yodeled cry of *whee-oodle, whee-oodle* will remain in memory long after the wetlands have dried. This impressive event, the artistry of flight augmented by the commanding quality of the cries, suggests spring flood acres. To hear these calls will charge the day with energy and meaning; they express the vigor and thrust of the season.

Not all of the great songs are heard in the day. Two night birds bring sounds of the wilderness to modern Ohio. The calls of the great horned and barred owls are as wild and romantic today as when they echoed from a wilderness, perhaps even more so by contrast. These night messengers sound their measured cadences at a time when there is little competition, hence the details are remembered. The heavy, low organ notes of the dignified great horned owl spell doom to many wildlife species. It is a powerful voice of the dark hours.

The higher eight-noted call of disk-face, the barred owl, has a more rollicking, humorous cadence, one that always brings a smile to the face of the listener. The eight-hooters are highly communicative; to hear a family calling antiphonally across a valley on a May evening is a rare privilege, whereas hearing them call from a deep swamp immediately before a summer storm may be alarming. The weird, unearthly shrieks and screeches are puzzling to the inexperienced but a joy to those who are familiar with the uncommon serenade.

And even the experienced are occasionally shocked. My old Ashtabula County friend was hunting coons one cold night. While he waited for the dog to strike a trail, he set his lantern inside a hollow stump, then leaned over it to get warm. Charlie remained in this position for a long time when suddenly from close overhead, there came a wild, maniacal scream. The hunter jumped to his feet, frightened by the wild cry so close at hand. Then he realized it was a barred owl. Apparently the bird saw the faint flickering of lantern light and couldn't fathom the scene. The owl left in a hurry when Charlie sprang up. Then the hunter was able to laugh. The somber contributions of these two large owls add to Ohio's great song of the earth.

Woodcock and jack snipe wing music are so strikingly different they should be included in the epic songs of the planet. The flight song of the woodcock is a sweet, delicate twittering suggestive of the small, intimate units of habitat they occupy. The cosmic sound of a winnowing jack snipe is on a grander scale, one suggesting the broad, high boundaries of the wide, open wetlands they inhabit. And to these great sounds, I would be tempted to add those of the wood thrush, the veery, and the white-throated sparrow.

Perhaps the most enjoyable duty I ever had as a game biologist was making woodcock singing ground counts. During the spring, woodcock flight songs grow in number as the population increases, then subside when the migration is complete and only resident birds remain. Woodcock singing ground counts usually begin in mid-April and continue through May when the nesting season ends. I ran these routes for many years, often accompanied by our children, whose keener hearing would account for birds I might have missed. The route would start when the first flight song of the evening was heard, usually about twenty minutes after sundown, and would continue for about one-half hour, the period when the light intensity was acceptable to singing male woodcock.

We would arrive early at the starting place, the site of a known singing ground. As we waited by a blooming patch of blueberries for the first flight song, the sights and sounds of the dying day came to us uninterrupted, the intimate sounds of nature. Woodcock were giving their nasal ground note, a bronx cheer, called a peent, which continued for several minutes before the first prenuptial flight song. American bitterns could be heard making their thunderpumping calls from distant swamps. Ducks and geese trafficked between feeding grounds and resting ponds. From marsh marigold-dotted swamps, swamp sparrows sang, and the last frantic alarm calls of robins and other daylight birds were heard. Then came the first flight song of the woodcock. The delicate, almost unearthly notes seemed as distant as the faint early stars that shone; they were somewhat like the fragile blossoms of the trailing arbutus then blooming; both were a reward for those who made the effort to observe them. The woodcock flight song was a sound that to me always denoted the precise end of day and the beginning of night. We listened for exactly two minutes, counting the number of singing male woodcock, then drove at least four-tenths of a mile to the next stop and repeated the process. Amphibian calls from woods ponds were so loud that occasionally listening points would have to be relocated.

While listening for a woodcock, the calls of many other birds came to us. We heard great horned and barred owls, whippoorwills, and the winnowing of snipe. I learned that there were far more whippoorwills in the area than I was aware of. Occasionally, before deep dark, we would observe an owl start on a hunting flight, accompanied by the young birds. But the greatest sound incidental to the census was the winnowing of snipe, mostly migrants although a few nested in the area. The weirdly beautiful sound came down out of the night sky regularly. Often on running a route, especially during the early season and particularly on stormy nights, a snipe would follow the car, winnowing from close overhead, for it must have dived low, apparently attracted by the motion of the only other visible sign of life and movement at the lonely site.

On the form I have before me, made on a May 2, sunset was at 8:26, it was overcast, the temperature was in the fifties, the wind about ten miles per hour by the Beaufort scale, and the moon was in the last phase—all information required to determine censusing conditions at the time. We made eight stops and located eleven occupied singing grounds. The entire experience was an esthetic adventure despite the fact that we were occasionally checked by law men who couldn't imagine any reason, unless an evil one, for standing along a roadside listening in the spring dusk.

The bubbling, compulsive birdsong is the ebullient, whimsical heart song of romantic May. As I ponder the marvels of the Song Moon, a question arises. Can man invent a one-half ounce musical machine that will migrate ten thousand uncharted miles yearly, constantly adjusting to changing, often hazardous conditions? The answer is the key to May's charms and a measure of nature's inventiveness.

In the heated pursuit of birds and wildflowers, observers often miss seeing the young mammals, which are becoming abundant at this time. A watchful birder might also see young red foxes gathered around the mouth of their home den during a warbler field trip, and very likely the vixen would be squalling a warning from some remote thicket. Young fox squirrels venture forth and become active on the home tree at this time. The young of most mammals are active and visible, so keep your eyes open while outdoors in May.

A Pike County friend once told me that when the maple samaras or winged seeds dry, usually starting in late May, the old timers in the hills knew that it was time to start hunting squirrels. This phenological relationship was important at a time when humans relied on nature for much of their sustenance.

In May, snapping turtles leave their watery haunts, traveling in search of sandy soil in which to deposit their ping-pong ball eggs. They cross roads and highways in this search and are more visible than at any other time of the year. This movement is most noticeable in the vicinity of extensive swamps and marshes, and the turtles commonly leave a muddy trail across the highway if they have just left the mud and water. I have enjoyed many fine dinners when I intercepted a snapping turtle crossing a highway. Other turtles move, too, especially after a rain. The sight of box turtles on the roads is a permanent feature in the hill counties.

Pollen-covered woods pools and ponds vibrate with the deafening clamor of amorous amphibians, even drowning out the great bird chorus. There are many tones to the outcry, but the most persuasive to me are the minor key toad trills; they always bring on a pensive spell. Here is another man's analysis of this

amphibian outpouring: chorus frogs utter an abrupt *kreek;*
peeper cry is high pitched; cricket frogs click; woods frogs quack;
American toads have a treble trill; Fowler's toads utter a lispy
buzz; tree toads supply the soprano; bull frogs rumble the bass,
and green frogs come up with an emphatic twang. Taken together with birdsong during the day and the insect chorus at
night, it creates a remarkable symphony or cacophony, depending
on the point of view.

May is the redman's Planting Moon. It is also the white
man's planting time, creating a great sense of urgency in the
man on the land: it is the month of heavy spring work, fitting
and planting through long, weary, dusty hours every dry day.
"Plant your corn when the dogwood is in bloom" goes a pleasant
old phenological saying, thus linking hard labor with bright
beauty. I recall sitting along newground fencerows in planting
moons of the past, waiting to tend the corn planter, and making
elder popguns to while away the time. It was pleasant sitting in
the sun with balmy breezes; dogwood blossoms were bright in
the woods, and the world never seemed younger. Later, when the
corn was up, the family would return to plant Kentucky Wonder
pole beans. Birdsong poured from the adjacent woods, toads
trilled from the woodland pools, and we boys would wander
through the field, planting beans when and where fancy dictated
despite mild parental protests.

Growing up on a farm and visiting its remote corners daily on
compulsive excursions, I seldom consciously noticed the constant
change that was taking place. Such awareness came only when I
had been absent for a week's visit to city relatives and returned
to find that while I was gone, the corn had grown beyond expectation. There were other changes marking the gradual transition in the yearly landscape, and for the first time, I believe, I
consciously became aware of the inexorable passing of time, and
that I had missed a stage in the season's progress. There is a
moral here: never let a season pass without keeping in regular
touch with it; otherwise you will harbor a sense of incomplete-
ness later.

Following corn planting, tobacco was set in soil fitted to garden texture. Setting and tending this tender crop meant much
exacting, difficult work. Now that little tobacco is grown, soybean

planting follows after corn is safely in the ground. Early hay may be made, helping to change the appearance of the landscape somewhat.

Somewhere in the busy May farm schedule, the truck patch would be planted. Usually a plot of newground soil would be saved for this purpose, and the planting and tending through the summer provided many adventures. The family Airedale would tree groundhogs or possums; a nest of bumblebees would be located to be cleaned out later by boys armed with shingle paddles. One important element is gone from modern farms. In the old days, it was customary to keep a few guineas or geese, or perhaps both; they constituted the security systems of those times. The appearance of a stranger was immediately made known by cackling guineas and honking geese. This would cause the family dog to investigate, so the system was far more efficient than might have been expected.

The greatest value from farming in those days was the strength gained from contact with the soil. Many persons forced from the land by economic trends attempt to regain this strength by getting outdoors to study nature or to hunt, fish, or harvest. For the forager, May is rich in wild treasures, but the morel mushrooms must rank at the top. An army of Buckeyes eagerly wait from one season to another for the privilege of hunting for these gourmet delicacies.

When hot, humid days occur in early May, members of this special fraternity of outdoor people grow restless until they are able to get out to roam the woodlands. This strong, irrational compulsion is known as morel madness, and when it hits, it is time to hunt the sponge mushroom. Once the morel hunters get in the woods, the charm of the quiet pursuit takes over, quiets their compulsion and, with success, brings contentment.

This compelling quest for morels gave me another sense of the passing of time. While hunting them, one is not immediately aware of the hours going by. But after hunting the same areas for many years, I became strongly conscious of time's effects. I remember many events by the setting in which they occur. Trees are important in morel hunting; I look under the same ash or dead elm tree year after year. Trees change slowly, but even they eventually show the passing of the years. Trees by which I once found morels are now dead and in some cases, no sign of them remains. It finally came to me that I had observed great changes in the woodlands; they were no longer the woods I had first known, but the intensity of my pursuit had blinded me to the change. The woods had matured and were now fully shading the ground; some were past their prime, and trees were dying or lost to storms. This long term awareness of time had even more impact than had childhood recollections of the progress of the corn crop during a one-week vacation away from the farm. It is another aspect of time, an entity with which I am more obsessed each passing year. This realization makes me even more appreciative of the value of the Indian moons as units of temporal measurement.

Mushroom hunters watch weather conditions as the season approaches. They speculate and calculate as to when the first morels will appear, for they don't want to miss out on these prizes. There are three choice kinds of morels. Earliest to appear are the black morels, the *morchella angusticeps* of the field books. They are found when the Juneberry is in full bloom, according to Alexander H. Smith, author of the *Mushroom Hunter's Field Guide*. They appear before leaves develop enough to shade the woods floor. At the same time, two less desirable types of mushroom appear: the early morel, which is toxic to some persons, and the half-free morel, so called because of the manner in which the cap is attached to the stem. The best of the lot is *morchella esculenta*, the sponge mushroom. According to Smith, this most popular morel appears when red oak leaves are in the mouse-ear stage, about ten days after the black morel appears. The last of the morels to pop up is the big-footed *morchella crassipes*, a giant in size with a large, thick stem. It follows the sponge mushroom by about ten days, and its appearance not only signals the end of the morel season, but also coincides with the emergence of ticks and mosquitoes. I find all of these morels in the same favorite spots, so apparently they occupy the same habitat.

Morels, like other mushrooms, are found where there is food. They cannot manufacture their own food; they live by breaking down organic material, especially woody substances. They reduce wood to humus. Wherever morels appear, rest assured that their food is present, and when temperature, moisture, and humidity are right, they will push up through soil and leaves. Aspect is important; they normally appear first on south-facing slopes where the sun first warms. As the season progresses, they can be found in other sites, such as north-facing slopes and in shady woods. I have found that east-facing slopes are especially productive.

Special sites where I concentrate my efforts include the base of gravelly hills, near seepage sites; all steep slopes where presumably the mycelium (the fungus plant on which mushrooms appear as fruit) surfaces; on hillsides at the level where groundhog dens occur (usually gravelly, well-drained sites); on slopes where dead leaves lodge against prostrate grapevines, fallen logs, or stumps that hold moisture; on burnt-over areas, and near dead elms. I pay special attention to snail and slug-infested, deep, damp gullies where wild ginger, jack-in-the-pulpit, and showy orchis bloom and ovenbirds nest. Whenever I find morels, I always hunt the area downwind, downgrade, or downstream where the spore might be carried by wind or water.

Morels are found in old orchards, in undisturbed woods, under ash trees or dead elms, in grapevine tangles, and along waterways where their spore has been washed. It takes time and experience to learn to see the morel pattern and to learn to know good, productive spots. Little wonder that morel hunters go to such extremes to keep their choice hunting grounds secret.

Every morel hunter has a special method of hunting, phenological reminders as to when they appear. In pioneer times, as Europeans came to a new land and explored across its breadth, they developed a set of memory props as to when to plant and harvest and perform other tasks important to survival. Since they were extremely busy just surviving, these phenological sayings made their difficult lives somewhat easier. They noticed, for example, that the early black morels popped up when Virginia bluebells first bloomed. The peak production of the yellow *esculenta* was expected when lilacs and apple trees blossomed, and when cranesbill began to fade, the morel season was nearly over. These bright, flowering plants were much easier to see than going afield every day to look for mushrooms, and the association saved much time and effort.

Morel season is purely a local situation with wide variation from one site to another, like a series of microclimates, which may be the case. Occasionally widespread favorable conditions occur during their fruiting season; then morels are to be found everywhere. Successful hunters range widely in their search; like a good bird dog, the wide ranger finds more of what he is looking for. Thoughtful hunters always carry morels in a mesh bag, one that allows the morel spore to be scattered through the woods to provide for the future.

Connoisseurs consider the morel to be the finest taste treat from the outdoors. Its flavor is distinctive and unforgettable. In the hills, they were called woods fish, apparently an effort to define their uncommon taste. Usually morels are sautéed in butter, and sherry wine may be added when they are almost done; they are cooked until the sherry has been absorbed. Chef Dieter of Columbus prepares a dish made with morels, wild rice, and crabmeat or shrimp that is the richest food I have ever eaten.

When more morels are found than can be immediately used, they should be dried on a screen in the sun or in a warm oven, or they may be strung and hung to dry. When thoroughly dry, they should be stored in an airtight container. Soak them in milk to restore to full size for cooking, and save the milk to make morel gravy, for it has absorbed the distinct flavor. Drying morels intensifies the flavor and is the ideal way to preserve these fine food items.

I have more difficulty finding mushrooms each year. This may be due to increased competition; it may be due to overharvesting or to carrying them in sacks that do not permit the spore to be spread. Morels were found around dead and dying elms for several years, and their hunters came to depend on this relationship. Now elm trees are less plentiful, and dying elms are rarely seen. Several years ago I would find two hundred or more morels each year; in late years I find only twenty-five or thirty, hunting the same areas. The morel situation is puzzling, but then, next year we might have a bumper crop.

Many other creatures consume morels. Snails and slugs feed on them. So do mice and chipmunks. But white-tailed deer appear to be the chief competitors of morel hunters. Deer tracks are plentiful in areas where mushrooms thrive and always seem to be there ahead of the morel hunter.

Fish are active in May; spawning occurs, and fishing is perhaps the best of the year. When the dogwood blooms, suckers are on the riffles; when blackberries bloom, bluegills may be taken on wet flies fished over beds of emerging aquatic vegetation; when dandelions star grassy fields, largemouth bass are hitting, and when the columbine blooms on Lake Erie island cliffs, the smallmouth bass run is at its peak around the islands. Follow a stream to fish like a May-crazed, carefree boy. Go unprepared except for a handline. Turn over streamside sod to find earthworms and grubs for bait. Fish through holes in spreading sycamore roots in the dark pools beneath where brightly colored butterbellies and red-eyed goggle-eyes hungrily seize the bait in a mad feeding spree. Perhaps a hefty smallmouth bass will grab the bait. String the fish on a thin willow branch stringer. You will become so completely involved in this truant pursuit that you will be reborn. Those fish from cool, springtime water will be the best you taste all summer. Walk the creek for frogs and turtles. Both offer some of the finest table fare to be found.

May's potherbs are among the best of the year. Pokeberry shoots (hillbilly asparagus) usually are tall enough—six to eight inches high—to be cut when the morel season is finished. Cooked like asparagus, they are very tasty. Cowslips or marsh marigold, mentioned earlier, may last into May; they are also excellent fare. I once enjoyed cowslip greens at a friend's home in Ashtabula. The greens, taken from a Pymatuning Creek swamp, were cooked with a ham bone, and the combination is excellent. Small glasses of the rich broth were served as appetizers.

Dandelion flowers are eaten by many wild food enthusiasts. Pick only the fresh, full flowers. For four servings, use the following recipe: two cups dandelion flowers, ⅔ cup cracker crumbs, one egg beaten, 2 tablespoons milk. Combine egg and milk. Dip the flowers into the batter, then into the cracker crumbs. Sauté in oil for one minute on each side and serve hot. It's one way to get rid of the dandelions in your lawn.

May is a time for the senses, when spring fever commonly reaches its most virulent state. It is vagabond time, time to steal away, to lose oneself in pursuit of pure romanticism. It has been said that the May hatch is an odd one. Many events of this fresh, different month support the contention. Follow your individual impulses on such a day to complete freedom from care. Be truant in May! Steal the time to wander all day viewing the natural wonders of the season. Days spent in May truancy are never lost; memories garnered then are the most treasured of a lifetime, so heed the compulsion to go home again. A line from an Oskar Strauss operetta perfectly describes the sentiment of the season: "to live again in May before everything is over."

An ideal way to enjoy the multiple May pastimes is to follow a smallmouth bass stream, wading upstream against the swift water in search of these scrappy game fish with soft craws, minnows, or artificial lures. Rest whenever a concentration of warblers is sighted, taking time to watch them. They aren't called the butterflies of the bird world for nothing. Also at this time, the bigfooted morels are poking through to light and warmth. A day spent in the pursuit of these big three May delights will establish the mood of the time.

In the past, the phenology of Decoration Day (now more commonly known as Memorial Day) was judged by the availability of flags, pineys, and snowballs, the local names for iris, peony, and hydrangea. If they were ready to be cut for grave decoration, the season was a normal one. Visiting cemeteries to decorate graves was a time for quiet remembrance. I'll never forget a scene I witnessed in Portage County. I was driving near Hiram on Decoration Day when I saw an elderly couple stopped at a small cemetery. Their horse was tied to a post, and they were carrying flowers from their buggy to decorate old, almost forgotten graves. This quiet event occurred in highly industrialized northeastern Ohio almost within sight of the tall, smoking, steel mill stacks. It impressed me far beyond the blaring bands and organized gatherings. These elderly people were decorating in quiet, sincere memory, unobserved by any but chance travelers on that lonely, remote road.

And after Decoration Day, things quieted down. It, not the solstice, was the beginning of summer to many. Planting was over, bird migration and the great thrust of plant growth were slowing or finished. The high sense of anticipation had passed with the dynamics of the month.

The events of May (as well as the other months) are the same year after year, yet they are always fresh and new because of seasonal change. But sometimes in the outdoors one comes upon a new scene or event that seems strangely familiar. This condition, known as déjà vu, has been described as an altered state of consciousness in which past experiences penetrate into the present mind. It has also been described as an illusion of memory in which one experiences a new scene or event as if it had been lived through before. Psychologists tell us that the subconscious mind often attempts to inform us for our own benefit. Is déjà vu an attempt of the subconscious mind to lead us to a better life by recalling pleasant states of the past? Such an experience commonly brings on a childlike simplicity during which one is honest, open, entirely without pretense. The outdoors is important to many as a way back to their tribal past, a return to a better, childlike self that was natural, honest, charitable. The Bible states that one can enter the kingdom of Heaven only as a child. Perhaps the déjà vu spell is an effort by the subconscious to lead the individual to happiness, to the carefree, childlike state attained when honestly enjoying nature—a state comparable to entering a heaven on earth.

May never arrives but what I recall Hoagy Carmichael's song, "One Morning in May"; I first heard the song during my own Maytime. It possesses all the magic of "Stardust" and has the same romantic appeal. The song is perfect for the time—a time of beauty and hope. There are none too many Mays in any lifetime, so we should make the most of each yearly pageant. This May, savor the delights of the fresh, dewey season. Gentle, natural uses of the earth's bounty are welcome; they do not harm the earth. Modern industrial progress, foreign to "honest nature's rule," is dooming man and the planet. It is time to return to simpler, sounder ways of living. Regular contact with nature is increasingly important to everyone—an essential way to achieve this goal of being ecologically kind to the earth and, ultimately, to ourselves.

June

June is a pleasant month despite the onset of summer's heat. What began in March and April reaches a peak in June. The mood and pleasantness of the month represents the high tide of the year; near perfect weather produces idyllic conditions, almost rivaling those of October. June days are *rare*, as James Russell Lowell so aptly stated.

Two-thirds of the month is spring astronomically; summer officially arrives at the solstice on or about June 20. Then the earth pauses, tilts, and reverses direction. June offers the best of the season passing, and of the one just starting. Within it is the longest day of the year—more than fifteen hours of daylight—before the sun starts moving southward again. During this calm period, it seems that the season's freshness will be retained beyond normal expectations, an illusion similar to that of Indian Summer.

As a boy, I used to judge the quality of the coming day by the sight of the sun on the white front porch pillars. If they were bright with sunlight when I awoke, the day seemed cheerful and well started. If it was cloudy, the pillars appeared dull, and I tried to go back to sleep.

Strong steady winds blow in June; these winds can surround an individual and completely isolate him with his thoughts. Then they may abruptly stop, and he returns to the immediate surroundings. Winds create a strange world of fantasy; trees bend and wave to create a dizzying, mesmeric effect; tawny fields of headed wheat become inland seas, waving and tossing endlessly as they are scanned by the wind. Cold spells occur but rarely during this pleasant month; in the folk language these are known as locust or blackberry winters, depending on which plant is blooming at the time the cold snap occurs. But despite these unusual spates of weather, June is a pleasing month, one which foretells the coming time when living will be easier.

During the leafy month of June, fluffy trees are filling as chlorophyll is pumped into the leaves, and by the month's end they will have a solid, glossy appearance, having reached full expansion. The green of the burgeoning universe of vegetation becomes dominant.

The wildflowers of the woodlands fade as the woods are plunged into leafy shade; those of the open areas bloom and come into prominence. Snakeroot does bloom in the woods, and in favored sites partridgeberry or twinflower's shy blossoms appear. The flowers of the fields include mustard (winter cress or rocket), whose yellow blooms dot wheat and oat fields; in times past farmers would send their sons out to pull them on wet mornings unsuited to other work. Other noticeable field flowers are mullein, wild carrot, and milkweed. Along streams, scouring rush is approaching the stage where it once was gathered and bundled by boys. It was then sold to housewives for a few pennies a bunch to be used to scour pots and pans.

The winds of June are often heavily freighted with the fragrance of the time: blooming clover fields, black locust groves, or the more subtle scents of wild rose, wild grape, or tiny basswood blossoms. The licorice smell of blooming elder clumps carries far. Most of these fragrances are more noticeable on cool, dewey nights.

In the woods, tulip poplar trees bloom; their tall, yellow, flame-shaped symmetry stands out. Some flowering dogwood flowers may last into June. Catalpa trees are blooming, and the cigars will follow. In the bottomland, blue wild iris flowers stand above the grasses. In quiet villages, freshly cut grass replaces the rural smell of newly mown hay, and mock orange and honeysuckle fragrance sweetens the yard and doorstep.

Perhaps the peak of birdsong is reached in early June as rich, full-throated, territorial songs ring out. Morning and evening birdsong is still strong in woodlots; the farm woodlots are still islands of bird music. But birds are nesting and rearing young and will soon be quieter. There are many young birds present in June; the steady hum of replenishment production is evident everywhere.

The wheezy, waterpipe music of veerys still sounds from the mosquito-infested swamp forests of northeastern Ohio, a tolling, siren song. There is the strong echo of woodpecker carpentry ringing through the woods. Turkey vultures nest in brushpiles or hollow logs. I once found a vulture's nest in such a log containing one fuzzy, white young. When we looked in at one end, the young vulture would race to the other end; its foot treads sounded like a racing horse in that sounding chamber. Young, blue-eyed crows are appearing; their incomplete caws mark them as immature. At this time, if one hoots like an owl, he will have every protective adult crow within hearing diving at and scolding him.

Upland plovers are scarce in Ohio today. Forty years ago they were plentiful, and their soft calls, interpreted by Morrow County farmers as saying "whippoorwill," was a common song. Their habit of holding their wings aloft after alighting, then carefully folding them into place, was always a delight to behold. It is my belief that pasture improvement has thinned their numbers; they prefer thin vegetation for nesting cover. The dense legume pastures, which are now common, doomed them to virtual extinction in this state. But the pasture improvement programs that caused upland plover decline brought about the tremendous increase in the redwing blackbird population. Dense legume growth provides optimum nesting conditions for redwings similar to those found in a cattail marsh.

Bobolinks and meadowlarks sing on the wing, a happy, bubbling song as they hover above meadows. The pure whistled calls of bobwhite quail ring from fence posts as they immodestly page themselves. Field sparrows call plaintively from blooming wild rose bowers, a combination of two examples of lonely, shy beauty. A pileated woodpecker flies from one woods to another; his high, undulating flight commands attention. Spectacular redheaded woodpeckers fly over open fields, feeding on the wing—an uncommon sight in my experience, and a habit much safer than flying across highways. Sadly they appear to be declining in number. Fewer roadside nesting sites and higher auto speed on the highways probably account for this decline. Cedar waxwings feast at a mulberry tree. Other fruit eaters gather at honeysuckle bushes to feed on the red ripe fruits.

Reverting fallow fields grown to wild cherry trees are alive with cuckoos feeding on tent caterpillars, which decorate the trees with their webs. Yellow-breasted chats sing through the June nights, inspired by the seasonal madness. Mother wood ducks keep careful watch on their young. A colony of rough-winged swallows flits about the bank nest holes, sweeping over the creek in a lively, erratic pattern. In the hills, whippoorwills' repetitive calls lace the June night, a memory-stirring sound.

Young mammals of the year are abundant and often entertaining. They are usually trusting and unafraid. One June day, a mouse-sized chipmunk scampered at my feet, peeking, then hiding as if playing a game. Young rabbits are seen everywhere. On an early morning or late evening drive in the country, several may be seen per mile.

The first of June is the peak of fawning in Ohio, a time to confine free-ranging dogs. Occasionally a farmer will find a fawn as he mows hay, and it will lie still, trusting to protective coloration to escape detection.

With young mammals so abundant, there is much dispersal travel as they move away from concentrations of their kind, and the traveling young are often victims of highway traffic. Young fox squirrels seem to be especially vulnerable. The heavy road kill results in large numbers of scavengers being seen along the highways—hawks, owls, vultures, crows, possums, and skunks.

With warmer weather, all living creatures are active, feeding and replenishing their kind. Snapping turtles still crawl from their watery habitat to travel in search of a place to deposit their tough-skinned eggs. They are still the most visible and vulnerable of any time of the year as they cross highways in their travel.

Box turtles always move following a rain, and in the hills they are a conspicuous sight as they crawl. Many a father stops to capture a young one to take home to his children; this may account for reports of box turtles throughout the state. Snakes feed on the abundant young of all kinds. In Shawnee State Forest, poison snake collectors are busy, capturing rattlesnakes and copperheads for sale to universities. One collector told me he always annoyed them so they would coil, then he would lift them with a pitchfork. Poisonous snakes are common enough in this area that snakebite victims aren't rare. Woods workers and berry pickers seem to be most vulnerable.

Fish spawn, and dark, moving masses of fry are a frequent sight in lakes, ponds, and creeks. The amphibians have finished mating and tadpoles show up in sluggish waters. At sundown, insects become lively and abundant. The night calls start in June, and they culminate in the overwhelming nocturnal chorus of late summer. Colorful butterflies appear to brighten the fields as they visit the wildflowers. Monarch butterflies hover above milkweeds. The big moths also appear, though they are seldom seen by the majority. These shy, large beauties are sometimes attracted with sugar water baits, and lunas, cecropias, and many others come to feed. In the past, many gardeners planted four o'clocks, pretty-by-nights, to attract moths. And appropriately, June bugs emerge to fly and bump into screens in their bumbling, awkward flight.

On the farm, the frantically busy time of fitting and planting is past; more peaceful pursuits occupy farmers. The powerful chlorophyllic surge is slowing except for the fertilized, cultivated crops.

The outdoor-oriented person has developed a high sense of anticipation during the dynamic spring season. Now that migration is long over and the early surge of plant growth is slowed, a letdown sets in. In the distant past, hoeing corn in June's delightful weather was an excellent way to ease the sense of the season's strong obligation through contact with the earth. This quiet task allowed time for thought, and the sensual impressions of nature filtered into subliminal awareness with little interference. The soft scents of the Sixth Month came to lighten the heart of the boy with the hoe—the honeyed sweetness of clover and black locust, and the more delicate redolences. The rich tapestry of birdsong from the shady, cool woods was dinned into memory and would replay throughout a lifetime as thoughts of youth surfaced. The call of a pewee always summons the image of a cool, shady woods on a hot summer day.

The cultivation of corn and tobacco with horse-drawn equipment was quiet, peaceful June work; the worker was near enough the ground to be able to watch for Indian artifacts. Finding an arrowhead always sent the mind back to the active days of the Wabash Indian Trail, a western Ohio landmark for centuries, and an important trail among Ohio's extensive network of ancient travel routes. Some of the greatest Indian leaders of the Northwest Territory traveled this portage between Lake Erie and the Ohio River watershed headwater streams. Later the armies of St. Clair and Wayne followed it as they marched north to fight the Indians. Many notorious frontiersmen also traveled the trail, so the finding of a projectile point, as they are now called, always stirred up thinking of the early days of historically rich western Ohio. The promise of a find gave life and zest to the hoeing and cultivation of row crops.

Corn grows from a few inches tall at the month's beginning to two feet by its end, and this growth starts to change the appearance of the land. Soybeans also start to hide the bare earth, but more slowly. Wheat turns from green to gold with maturity, and it will be near a harvest stage by the month's end. Oat fields are whitening to a gray-green color. A subtle purple haze overlays blooming timothy fields, and clover is bright and sweet with blossom. Blooming clover heralds the start of haymaking; then the "sweet grass" fragrance of curing hay fills the air. An Ohio man who moved to the suburban east coast lamented that the earthy aroma of his rural habitat was missing from his new environment, especially the fragrance of newly mown hay.

The June cadence is that of lowing cattle, bleating sheep, and frisky calves and lambs. On June nights, a hen will lose her balance on the roost and flap frantically to regain her perch. This noise often sets dogs to howling, especially on moonlit nights when they are likely seeking a reason to howl, and other dogs take up the howling out of hearing. In the Ohio River counties, the deep, resonant, organ-notes of steamboat whistles moan, an unexpected sound to visitors as it echoes in the wild, wooded valleys away from the river.

Farm families, sitting on the front porch, will see a mother skunk lead her black and white line of kittens forth to forage; they will hear chilling screech owl calls from yard trees and the last worried alarm calls of birds as night settles in. Late in the month, fireflies emerge and add their soft, semaphoric, flashing lights to the peaceful scene.

Gardens start to yield. The first meal of new peas and tiny new potatoes may be enjoyed. Old fashioned gardens always had gooseberries growing along the fence, along with rhubarb and currants. Perhaps the first fresh gooseberry pie of the year appears on the table in late June. Cherries ripen and attract robins, red-headed woodpeckers, and other fruit eaters. Most distinctive of all is the sight of a family of cedar waxwings lined up on a wire by a cherry tree. The bird nearest the tree picks a cherry and passes it to the neighbor; the cherry is passed down the row to the last member of the family group in a gentle, polite ceremony. This is one of the rewarding social sights awaiting June bird-watchers.

June's wild harvest is not especially abundant, but it is pleasant for newness, for quality, and for berries! Juneberries rightfully come to fullness this month, the first fresh, wild pie timber of the year. June was the Strawberry Moon of the Indians. What a delightful way to welcome the fruitful season after a severe winter! Wild strawberries have a tartness and delicacy of taste found in few other fruits; they are far and away the outstanding wild fruit of the month. Black raspberries ripen late in the month in fencerows where wheat shockers and hay pitchers used to enjoy them. The uncommon thimbleberry or purple flowering raspberry grows in northern sites in Ohio. The fruit is not outstanding, but the large, purple-rose blossoms are a treat to behold. Mulberries ripen and attract all the fruit-eating birds of the community to the dismay of the housewife who hangs out a washing to dry. Pawpaws one inch long promise rich food for man and beast in four month's time. If there has been adequate rainfall, there may be oyster mushrooms. For tea connoisseurs, June has always been a proper time to gather and dry wild tea plants. These include ditany, New Jersey tea, various mints, yarrow, and basswood blossoms.

Elderberries offer more than foamy white blossoms and fruit for pies and wine. When they are blooming, elderberry blossom fritters are a tasty, delicately flavored treat. Pick the flowers at the height of bloom, remove the coarse stems, and dip the flower clusters in a batter made up of one cup of flour, one tablespoon of sugar, one teaspoon of baking powder, two eggs, and one-half cup of milk. Wine may be added to this batter. Fry the dipped clusters in deep fat at 375 degrees for about four minutes or until they are a golden brown. Place them on a paper towel, squeeze a little orange juice over them, roll in granulated sugar, and serve hot.

When blackberries are in bloom, it is time to fly fish for large bluegills by fishing wet flies over emerging aquatic weed beds. Fly fishing in a June twilight is one of the most peaceful pursuits imaginable. In the quiet dusk, all the sounds of an awakening nocturnal nature come without interference. The sounds of the dying day join with the cadences of emerging night life. Coons, minks, and muskrats may come to hunt the waterway.

When red clover is blooming, the big channel catfish run is on in Sandusky Bay. The white bass run coincides with the channel cat run, so there is plenty of opportunity for Lake Erie anglers. Turtle hunters may be seen wading creeks on mild, sunny June days, bending to explore muskrat dens and other underwater holes with their trained hands, feeling for the hard shells of snapping turtles. It's a hazardous occupation, but the rewards are great: fried turtle or soup.

And as always, small boys fish in the warm sun, watching a snakefeeder perched on their bobbers, hoping that a sudden bite will give the insect a bath.

Ben Logan, in his book, *The Land Remembers*, tells of man's origin as a creature of the earth, and how in recent decades of "progress" he has forsaken the earth and its ways. The author relates the Greek myth of Antaeus, who was invincible as long as he retained contact with his mother, Gaea, the earth. His defeat came from Hercules, who held him away from the earth. The obvious lesson is that modern man, kept from the living earth by occupational and societal demands, starves in many ways, and as a result is less useful to society. The moral is, retain your contacts with the earth!

During the distinctive atmosphere of the June lull, take time to notice the beauties of this idyllic month. Farm families used to do this by taking a picnic basket to the woods while June wildflowers were brightening the scene.

In Ernest Thompson Seton's book for boys, *Rolf in the Woods*, Quonab, the old Indian, is listening to wild, moving, night music that "seems to come from the stars." The boy Rolf asks him what it is. "That was the mystery song of someone. I never saw him," Quonab replies anthropomorphically. This simple account of an unknown sound of nature and its mysterious fascination to the listener points up the value of the unknown to nature observers. They spend a lifetime learning the secrets of nature, yet an unknown sound often brings a dimension of pleasure much greater than the familiar.

With warm days and cool nights, dooryard evergreens give off a strong fragrance reminiscent of northern conifer forests. The start of the summer night chorus—a haunting, timeless sound— lends a mysterious dimension to the night, and to the month. Mother Nature is a siren, mystic voice.

June is so peaceful it seems that it will last forever; sadly it won't. The month is largely dominated by fresh, tender aspects, but, like the foliage, it hardens into summer by the month's end. Still, the Sixth Month is an excellent time to remember the warning inherent in the myth of Antaeus. Get outdoors to maintain your contacts with the living earth, the source of life and strength. The blessings of June offer peace and contentment to those who seek their lasting values.

July

July is the first full month of summer, yet it comprises the heart of the summer season with its dog days intensity of heat and humidity. It was known to the Indian tribes as the Thunder Moon or the Heat Moon. How much more meaningful are these names of Indian origin than is the name July? Any meaning or beauty we have developed for our private names of the months comes from association; it is the condition or mood of the time which gives it value. The Indians went right to the heart of feeling; their subjective names have permanent significance, moon names that still carry the full meaning of the months.

What values would we preserve for the future if we were to name the moons today? Would we choose those of timeless beauty as did the morning mower in Robert Frost's poem "The Tuft of Flowers," who left a tuft of flowers that the mower of the afternoon sees? He left the one message that withstands the test of time: inherent, individual beauty. This permanence is characteristic of the Indian moon names. It takes an artist with a touch of the romantic to intuitively know what is permanent.

During the Thunder Moon, the great summer storms build up and roll across the land. Rural people will run out to stand in the rain, finding delightful, tactile pleasure in the caress of the raindrops and the cooling breeze the rain brings.

Summer was front porch time in a more relaxed and casual past. Families would gather there to spend long summer evenings, conversing in low tones against the mighty night song of the earth. The farmer would watch sheet lightning play on the western skyline, studying it for signs of a needed rain. If the northern lights flashed in the sky, the family was certain to witness the heavenly manifestation, always in the humble spirit with which they accepted anything that came from above. They would observe the Milky Way and the constellations with the same interest and reverence they reserved for the northern lights. Appreciation was the key attitude shown by these hardworking, honest individuals; the front porch was the place to sense the month's shaping up.

In July, just the start of summer, events are already pointing to autumn. At the start of the month, tree foliage, which has attained the solid, glossy look, indicates that it has reached its full growth for the season, until drought and the chemistry of autumn changes its appearance. Summer gardens are beginning to display their brightness. Hollyhock blooms climb the stalks as summer strengthens.

Sourwood and perhaps late basswood blossoms sweeten the air and the hives of busy honeybees this month. Dry maple samaras are still falling or being eaten by squirrels. Beechnut burrs change from green to gold. Dusty roadside vegetation was a characteristic of summer in the days before every road was hardsurfaced; it was white with road dust. But the outstanding feature of summer vegetation is the tall, bright wildflowers; they seem to reflect the bright energy of the day star in their blossoms.

Fields of chicory are a blue haze, perhaps dotted with oxeye daisies, Queen Anne's lace, and black-eyed susans. Joe Pye weed, teasel, sunflowers, magenta and yellow ironweed, and the striking orange of butterflyweed are noticeable. Milkweeds are fueling monarch butterflies to a future. Rarely the beautiful Michigan and Canada lilies are found. July was the Moon of Red Lilies to the Sioux. Purple loosestrife blooms in moist sites, and the extensive Lake Erie marshes begin to show color with pink mallow bloom. One of the most effective bouquets I remember was a bouquet of summer simples—chicory, Queen Anne's lace, and black-eyed susans—put in a simple vase by an old country woman of my acquaintance. She had true appreciation of beauty whenever it occurred.

July birds are quieter than during the nesting and rearing season. Now their tones are more parental as they strive to bring fledglings through the perilous, predatory time to maturity. Late in the month, they will molt and be private for a time. To the Cree and Ojibway, July is the Moon When Birds Cast Their Feathers.

There are a few good songsters active during the month. The wood thrush flutes his fine phrases morning and evening. From thick, brushy thrasher-haunt comes the rhyming couplets of brown thrasher mimicry—beautiful, distinctive, and doubly appreciated in July when birdsong is diminished from the peak spring months. The catbird's squeaky efforts are also heard. In brushy lots, indigo buntings and northern yellowthroats call. Woodlands ring with the crested flycatcher's imperative *wheep* or the non-stop phrases of the preacher, the red-eyed vireo. Robins may sing their carols in yards, and house wrens utter their bubbly chant. Flickers yammer or give their *skleer* cry, and they perform their unique anting ritual on lawns. Hummingbirds visit trumpetvines to probe the deep-throated orange flowers for nectar. Rain crows call for rain.

Goldfinches gather in thistle-blown fields; cedar waxwings feed at fruit trees or on insects over water; swallows gather with their young on utility wires; killdeer families utter their weary lament as they fly over moonlit fields. Nighthawks sweep the sky; flying against a new moon in a late afternoon blue sky, they are somehow a highly romantic sight.

Bobwhite quail still sing their name phrase from fence posts. Green herons squawk as they fly up creeks, a typical summer sound. In the large marshes, ducks molt and for a time are less visible. The month has been called "whippoorwilled July" in the hills where these birds are most common. But perhaps the most predictive bit of behavior is the gathering of large flocks of blackbirds containing many young of the year flying about the landscape; it foretells the coming of autumn, even as summer is just beginning.

The mammal population is at or near its high for the year; young mammals are everywhere, and predation is high as the carnivores kill to feed their young. The highway kill is also high as the young continue their dispersal movement into new territory. Many new woodchuck dens show up in fencerows as piles of fresh, damp earth.

In rural Darke County where I grew up, the appearance of rare or unknown wildlife was of interest to the entire population; the big event would freshen the currents of community conversation for many days. Much uncommon wildlife behavior can be observed in July. I saw two red foxes running and leaping high above the fresh oats stubble just after harvest, reveling in the clearer vision that shorter cover permitted. Occasionally white-tailed fawns will be discovered in hay or small grain fields; they bear the pattern of the Pleiades on their rumps at a time when this constellation is visible in the early morning July sky. The uncommon jumping mouse may rarely be observed when vegetation is cut on sandy or gravelly knolls, and young flying squirrels are making their first timid ventures through the air. One dusk on a red oak knoll near Wooster, the Izaak Walton group I was with became aware of activity in the trees but couldn't place it until a flying squirrel was seen planing from one tree to another. Until a glider was observed, this quiet activity had been going on with only a faint hint of its presence. We watched as long as light permitted.

Other forms of life are active, too. Perhaps the insects are most dominant because of their number and their behavior in relation to humans. The annoying insects keep us alert. We never venture outdoors without protection against mosquitoes, chiggers, or ticks. Houseflies force us to screen our homes. Yellow jackets attend our picnics and keep us uneasy.

June bugs have always been humorous insects to me. I recall many sleepy nights when bungling June bugs bumped against the windows, making me thankful I was protected from the insect hordes on the other side of the screen. Click beetles were objects of humor and entertainment in a distant past. Boys would collect them from dead wood and place them in a tin can. Whenever the beetles snapped their hinged bodies, they would bang around in the can—a mild and simple form of entertainment in the days when it had to be provided by the entertained! What a great time to be a boy!

I could never decide whether dung beetles were to be classed as humorous or acrobatic insects. When they roll the dung balls containing their hope for the future over a grassy plot, they perform acrobatic feats by standing on their heads and pushing with their hind legs. They were commonly called tumble bugs, among other names. Farm boys, upon spotting a pair so engaged, would plop down on their stomachs to watch the industrious beetles labor over the uneven surface. The aerial antics of grasshoppers were also considered entertaining. A grasshopper clinging to a stem of grass can perform a number of gymnastic feats just trying to steady his perch.

Horseflies, known as bonepickers in the old days, also provided some amusement. Boys would capture them and insert bluegrass seed head plumes into their rear ends, then release the bugs to hear them buzz loudly as they flew away. Occasionally one would be released in church to liven up the service. This cruelty was justified by the fact that horsefly bites are extremely painful to horses, sometimes causing them to run away while hitched to farm machinery.

July is host to a number of beautiful insects—the butterflies and moths. These brightly colored creatures command wide attention as they dance over garden and meadow, visiting flowers. Iridescent beetles of many colors also provide beauty for the person working close to the soil. But perhaps the givers of most romance and beauty are the fireflies. Has there ever been a child who didn't run through the dusk, pursuing and catching fireflies to keep in a bottle—a living light for a few hours? Fireflies have brightened summer evenings since long before man first looked at their coded messages of romance. Insects add much to our existence, not always to our liking, but they do keep us alert and interested.

The amphibian mating clamor has quieted by now. In July the frogs and toads respond largely to atmospheric pressure; the volume of their night cries now varies according to the weather. Added to the insect night sound, the total effect is to create a pulsing cadence that indicates the richness and health of the land. On hot, humid July nights, noises from a thousand species of living things moving through the lushness of summer's vegetative growth, calling each to its kind, swell to a chorus that permeates the being of all listeners. Insects of many kinds saw, scrape, rub, and vibrate to make their distinctive sounds, which merge into a pulsing crescendo. Along with this rhythmic beat are the special effects of the amphibians—lisps, trills, calls of many tones given in minor keys; this combined with the bullfrog boom and the yelp and twang of smaller frogs creates a haunting, continuous night song imprinting the subconscious mind until, awake or asleep, the listener is saturated with the vital forces of the summer earth.

The reptiles become fully active during the hot weather; in the hills the presence of copperheads and rattlesnakes make caution a valuable trait. Turtles crawl following a heavy rain. Trotliners set their lines in the lakes and big rivers to take the giant catfish, which become active feeders after a rain.

Traditionally, wheat was cut and shocked by July 4; oats was in the shock ten days later. Shocked wheat and oats stood darkly on moonlit nights, disappearing in the indistinctness of moonlight. Now grainfields are standing in the morning; by night they have been combined, and only the strong, distinctive fragrance of new straw remains to remind that it had been a field of grain.

The Fourth of July was a lonely day on the farm when I was a boy. Not many farmers observed the holiday during the rural depression of the 1920s, although there were usually fewer farmers in the fields. Rarely did our family go away for the holiday; there were a few firecrackers, perhaps a Roman candle or a sky rocket, then a quiet evening on the front porch listening to the nighttime chorus.

In times past, the months of July and August were the heart of the threshing season. A farmer would spend every dry day away from home helping his neighbors thresh in exchange for the help necessary to get his own grain threshed. The work was hot, dusty, and exhausting, even to a man accustomed to hard work. The grain wagons would be lined up at the elevator waiting to be weighed and unloaded; it was a time of social opportunity.

One of the big rewards, especially to boys and younger men, was the threshing dinner. The sunbonneted women of the community would outdo themselves in striving to have the most lavish outlay of food to be found in the threshing ring, for by then garden and chicken yard provided amply for a well-filled table.

One July activity that made a strong impression on the community was the hauling of manure to clear the barnyard for the new straw stack; its fragrance hung in the night air and was often frowned upon. Yet many who frowned at it then now realize that its scent was much less offensive than the industrial fumes which fill the air and pollute the universe today.

The second cutting of hay, the rowen of New England, is often made in July, and the bouquet of drying hay is a gift to those on the land. There are many distinctive, strong scents in July—corn pollen, wheat straw, pungent horseweed pollen, swamp miasma on cool nights, sycamore balm in the bottomlands; all are scents that tease the memory of those close to the land.

In tobacco country, the hoeing and cultivation of tobacco demands attention; if tobacco caterpillars are plentiful, it is necessary to remove them by hand or to spray with paris green. But it is corn which dominates the land. It is "knee high and laid by" at the start of July; by month's end it is head high and bearing silk and tassels. During dog days weather, the quick growth of corn causes a constant rustle in the fields as the leaves thrust upward; the rustle is so noticeable that it suggests a breeze even on the stillest night. By the end of July, the corn is tall and pollinating, and the heavy, sweet, cloying scent on the air keeps humans swallowing hard. One caught in a cornfield as a rain moves across the land will hear the roar of raindrops hitting the leaves as the storm moves toward him, a distinctive sound of summer in corn country. I recall that boys were pleased when corn grew tall enough to hide their movements. Then it was possible to steal away to fish or swim, for being out of sight was to be out of mind when parents planned work.

The first comb honey of the season appears on July tables; usually it is clover honey, a favorite of rural communities. Also at this time, truck patches begin to yield heavily—the start of abundance. Sweet corn is the big treat, and late in the month strong-scented, orange-colored muskmelons ripen. It used to be a common practice to invite neighbors to the front porch during melon time to share this rich fare as families talked in the cool evening. It was also common for the young bucks to raid melon patches, often taking their booty to the creek swimming hole for a feast following a refreshing swim.

The first Ohio peaches ripen in July, and harvest apples ripen and appear on tables as tasty, piquant applesauce. Daily feasting

on garden and orchard plenty may lead to what country folk re-
fer to as the harvest plague, a seasonal hazard.

There is the start of opulence in wild nature, as well. The wild
harvest gains in volume as summer heat and light accumulates
on vine, bush, and tree. A few late Juneberries may still be available in protected sites in early July. Other fruits and berries
ripen. Black raspberries mature in fencerows. Blackberries, the
most abundant wild berry, ripen later. Picking blackberries requires Spartan courage; arms and neck are severely scratched,
and usually the harvester acquires a bad case of chiggers. Wild
cherries come of age; they serve primarily as food for the
wildlings. Their seeds appear in the droppings of many mammals
and birds. July was the Plains Indians' Moon When Cherries
Turn Ripe.

But the berry I remember most vividly is one I never tasted
until I was well past one-and-twenty. Blueberries were a sacred
food to me from early youth; they were akin to the brightly
colored storybook sugarplums of childhood in my mind. This
fascination came from reading James Oliver Curwood's novels of
the far north. Curwood wrote of blueberries repeatedly and en-
thusiastically, emphasizing their importance to man and beast in
the north country, especially on burnt-over land where enor-
mous crops of this delicious berry followed a fire.

When I moved to northeastern Ohio in the late 1930s, wild
blueberries were widely found. In the morainic kettlehole swamp
region, they grew in the swamps with buttonbush. The bushes
attained great size, often being ten feet tall, and they produced
abundantly. It was the practice to sell picking rights; a person
could pick all day for one or two dollars. The Amish of Geauga
County were regular customers; their buggies would arrive at
daybreak and leave at dusk, loaded with milk pails filled with the
deeply colored berries.

Wildlife was plentiful and varied in the blueberry swamps.
Berry pickers often flushed ruffed grouse and woodcock, and
smaller birds were plentiful, especially the fruit eaters. Occasionally the pickers would encounter a massasauga rattlesnake.

Blueberries also grew well in the reverting wet fields common
to much of northeastern Ohio. Ashtabula County had some extensive blueberry fields, but I fear that clearing and drainage may

have eliminated them. Picking blueberries in those lonely, brushy fields was a still, absorbing task; it was so quiet that one lost all sense of time while exercising the provider instinct. Those evenings in the blueberry fields created unforgettable memories.

The blueberries I picked were fully as good as I had imagined they would be; this is one of the few times in my life that reality equalled or even exceeded imagination. A pie made from freshly picked blueberries is one of the finest desserts, rivaling a northern spy apple pie for taste. And a deep orange, fragrant muskmelon half filled with complementary colored blueberries is as appealing to the eye as to the palate.

What is the strong appeal of blueberries? They are smooth, firm, and sweet, virtually seedless and not messy to pick. They possess a highly distinctive flavor, a deep blue color masked by a light dusty bloom, and they have a long life on or off the bush. They are high in energy and low in calories. Little wonder that the reality of blueberries lived up to the magic with which early reading had invested them. And little wonder that blueberry fields became enchanted, wildlife-filled areas for me.

July was known as the Blueberry Moon to some northern tribes. The appearance of ripe blueberries marked the start of welcome summer. Although their appearance is still a fine way to begin the season, there are other goodies for the gatherer of wild provender. The highly prized chanterelle mushrooms appear in July. The color of dried apricots, they carry a faint scent of that fruit. In France, chanterelles are treasured and expensive; here few mushroom hunters know or seek them.

Salsify or goatsbeard is grown in gardens, and soup is made from the oyster-flavored roots. Much salsify grows in the wild, often along roads, and it is easily recognized by the fluffy, tan-colored seed heads, similar to dandelion seed heads but larger.

The strong sense of harvest which reaches its peak in the autumn is first noticed in July. The fast growth of crops, their maturity and fruition, and the start of the autumn bird migration all foretell change and help to establish mood as summer is now well started. The immediate mood may be established as a cow bawls in a high, hoarse tenor for a newly weaned calf, by the snuffling of a herd of grazing cattle in the night, or by the bleating of a flock of sheep.

An endless array of plant and animal actors march across the July landscape, succeeding one another to create a sense of almost imperceptible change. Birdcalls are parental. Cicadas are starting their strident buzzing on sultry days. The great swelling chorus of night sounds pulses; the calls of insects and amphibians rule the darkness. Occasionally the squall of coon or fox, or perhaps the squawk of a heron or the scream of an owl flying through the night, sounds over the nocturnal chorus. Mysterious cries in the night are a feature of summer; they do much to establish the special mood of the season. In earlier times, almost every night through the warm season front porch families heard some unknown cry. It stimulated the imagination and set the mind to exploring new channels. On hot evenings there would be distant shouts from the creek swimming hole.

Evenings of peaceful front porch visiting against the pulsing nocturnal chorus—the cardiogram of a healthy land—transports the listeners to the distant past. And then the thud of a falling harvest apple brings them back to the present.

August

August starts with the dog days, a forty-day period in July and August when the Dog Star rises with the sun—a time of sweltering days and nights when corn grows best and humans suffer most. In times past, the dog days were regarded with apprehension because of the ancient fear of disease and discomfort. Dogs were said to go mad then. Boys couldn't swim in the creek because of the danger of disease and infection from the evil influence of the star. It was a fearful, forboding time, one heavy with superstition.

Sometime in August, the Thunder or Heat Moon sends a storm from the west to break the hot spell. Light colored clouds gather and build into a dark, blue-black mass that covers the entire western sky. Distant thunder and lightning announce the coming of the storm long before it strikes.

Giant, wind-driven thunderheads roll and tumble through the wild sky, and trees bend dangerously before the savage wind. When the powerful, jolting storm arrives, rain pours, lightning flashes close by, and thunder crashes and rumbles in a frightening demonstration of the fierce force of a Thunder Moon storm. But the fear-inspiring storm brings much needed rain to the corn and assures a good crop. And following the storm, a bright, many-colored rainbow can be seen, a reminder to those on the land of the eternal promise.

August is dependably hot and humid much of the time, yet late in the month, after the dog days, the lengthening nights will be cooler; then comes the green-gold days, a delightful cool spell so predictive of autumn. During this unusual time, temperatures

are cool or cold, days are sunny, and the late summer sun shining through the green world of vegetation creates a luminous
green-gold world and a mood as original as the conditions. This
time and this mood, each as distinctive as Indian Summer, are
anticipated by those who recognize it as an uncommon interlude
in the usual order of affairs. It has been said that these days are
stolen from the best of September. During this break in season,
the fullness of August's harvest is especially enjoyable. Often
the cool night breezes from organically rich bottomlands are
strong with pungent organic scent, a typical late summer and
early autumn redolence.

When the green-gold days arrive, cattail heads are mature. In
the distant past, they would be cut with long stems and the
fluffy heads soaked in kerosene. On a cool evening, the heads
would be set on fire, and children would parade with them until
they burned out. This pastime is reminiscent of the illuminations
of pioneer times when large bonfires were built just to liven and
brighten the dark scene.

August is a dry month despite the occasional storms, perhaps because of the heavy demand for water by the wealth of
vegetative growth that makes up our temperate region. But
the dry landscape is dotted with the tall, bright, late summer
wildflowers. They are chiefly of two colors, yellow and blue-
purple.

Yellow is the predominant color. Wild sunflowers are yellow,
as are the blooms of goldenrod, jewelweed, mullein, evening
primrose, butterflyweed, prairie dock, and yellow ironweed. In
eastern Ohio, the uncommon Canada lily is orange-red; in western Ohio, the Michigan lily is orange. Blue-purple is found in
the magenta ironweed, chicory, asters, teasel, lobelias, gentians,
and the head and stems of bluestem prairie grass, which Willa
Cather described as being the color of wine stains.

In wet woodlands, the blazing beauty of the cardinal flower
attracts attention. Boneset frosts the bottomlands, and in kettlehole swamps, buttonbush honey balls still attract honeybees.
Fallow areas of rich soil support a lush stand of head-high
horseweed. Joe Pye weed grows a man-and-a-half high. Pink and
white smartweed flowers appear in damp sites, contrasting pret-
tily with the copper-colored leaves.

The first autumn leaf color shows up in August. Sour gum (pepperidge in northeastern Ohio), sumac, and woodbine leaves are turning red. Basswood seeds helicopter to earth. Bittersweet berries start to turn orange late in the month. In southern Ohio, vining honeysuckle covers entire hillsides; its blossoms flood the valleys with nectareous sweetness. Trampled streamside mint gives off memory-haunting fragrance.

Birdsong has quieted in August; many birds are molting, and soon they will start the great southward movement. There are a few songsters still singing; catbirds mew, pewees sound their name, brown thrashers roll out their rhyming phrases, and wood thrushes flute. The most noticeable birds are the large flocks of blackbirds, which settle into cornfields to feed, and at evening fly to roost in village shade trees. This traditionally brought out the shotgun brigade to scare them away, for the flock whitewashed streets, sidewalks, and automobiles. Near the Lake Erie marshes, blackbirds become destructive; carbide exploding noisemakers are used to keep them away from cornfields. A major reason for the dramatic increase in icteridae numbers and the consequent crop damage was the pasture improvement program. This program resulted in dense, lush, legume fields, which created near ideal nesting conditions for red-winged blackbirds.

The night hawk migration largely occurs in late August; these graceful birds are a familiar sight to those on the land as they sweep the afternoon and evening skies. Often they will concentrate on insect flights just above the corn tops; some of the largest flights I have ever seen were of this type.

Doves flock to feed in harvested grainfields. Chimney swifts start to gather around large chimneys late in the month, and the sight of a large swirl of the twittering birds pouring into these structures at dusk is impressive. Shorebirds are already migrating, and shores and mudflats are alive with them. Teal and other early migrating ducks arrive in Ohio in August.

Where the thistledown blows, there you will find goldfinch flocks in August. Oddly, some are still nesting even as the autumn migration begins. Cedar waxwings are feeding in the willows. Long-tailed grackles are hunting crayfish in the shallow streams, hopping from stone to stone as they work the water, enjoying their catch on the rocks. The woodlands are noisy as crows worry hawks and owls, a continuation of their ancient antagonism.

In late August, turkey vultures gather again by the rivers at traditional roosting sites. There, on cool mornings, they will be distributed over the ground and on every fence post and tree, waiting with outstretched wings for the heat of the sun to dry their pinions and create thermal updrafts on which they will ride into the sky to scan the countryside. With spread wings, their profile resembles that of the legendary thunderbird. The sight of these sun worshippers is almost a primordial image; it would not have seemed out of place an eon ago.

The mammal population continues to be high, although predation is steadily reducing it. Many mammals are in or near cornfields. Corn is in the milk stage and is feasted upon by raccoons, woodchucks, squirrels, muskrats, beavers, and lesser forms. The head-high corn provides excellent cover; rabbits, foxes, deer, and other wildlife take refuge there as tracks in the soil will disclose. Sit down in a cornfield and wait; you will be surprised at the wildlife you will see if you are patient.

Even in the past when cover was more plentiful, corn cover was widely used. Woodlots were then grazed more so than today. Following World War I, the wide, brushy fencerows then so common were being cleared, destroying excellent wildlife cover and forcing wildlife into the woods, wetlands, and cornfields. Roadsides were not mowed so thoroughly then, and railroad right-of-ways provided excellent cover lanes. Fields of shocked corn often stood all winter to provide cover and food, in sharp contrast with the modern practice of plowing a field as soon as it has been harvested, turning under waste grain and cover.

The woodlots are astir in August. Squirrels are busy feeding on the new nut crop. Chipmunks have increased their clucking note, the most characteristic sound in the woods from now until winter. One mammal inspired a certain amount of apprehension in rural western Ohio. In my community, an old, neglected cemetery was overrun with thirteen-striped spermophiles, locally called gophers. They had dug extensive burrows in this remote old plot grown to weeds and yucca, and there were rumors that the gophers dug up human bones. The implication was that there was malicious intent in their digging, and many older women shuddered at mention of the cemetery and its mammalian inhabitants.

Other life forms are busy, too, as summer draws to a close. In the hills, box turtles are still moving with a change in the weather and are regularly seen on the highways. Snakes wait for their prey in blackberry thickets. Creek bank walkers find the punctured eggshells of snapping turtles where they have been dug up and eaten by raccoons and skunks.

Insects dominate August. The hot, humid weather of dog days creates ideal conditions for insect calls; the sleepless nights vibrate with a variety of metronomic sounds from the insect throngs, which combine to create a pulsing heartbeat of the land through the night. Cricket trill is fast and constant from fencerows and weedy fields. The flailing flight of a praying mantis along a fencerow tells that it is hunting insect prey. Monarch butterflies start their southward drift, and woolly worms are seen crawling across highways, all early signs of the approaching season.

August was the Maize or Green Corn Moon to many Indian tribes, a tribute to the importance of corn, one of the great gifts to humanity. The week-long August Green Corn dance of midwestern Indians celebrated the importance of this crop to Indian diets. Western tribes observed their ancient fertility rites when the heavy fragrance of corn pollen dominated the land, certainly an honest symbol for the ceremony. But, valuable as agriculture was to the Indians, giving them security through the lean, cold months, it also helped reduce them to a more sedentary status, a questionable influence on the wild, proud spirits as seen in historical perspective. The renowned Shoshone chief Washaki, known as a friend of the white man, understood this when he replied to the military men who urged his tribe to grow potatoes: "God damn a potato!"

Corn still dominates the fat farmland of the Midwest. During early August, pollination is still taking place, and the cloying scent is so dominant it chokes one. Corn ears are but tassels at the start of the month; by month's end they are well developed and husks are drying. One who drives through the better corn-growing counties after mid-August in a good year will be impressed by the endless miles of tall, deeply colored stalks bordering the road. The roads are canyons through the corn, broken occasionally by soybean prairies. These two crops dominate the landscape of the rich counties. In fact, in corn county, the fields shut off the ground air currents during the hot, humid time when they would be most welcome. They also shut off the view of the community, imposing a certain sense of isolation. Auto wrecks commonly happen at blind crossroads surrounded by corn.

Walking in a field of tall corn is a new experience for a person accustomed to open land; it is like being lost in a jungle. There are stories of men who became lost in the middle of a large corn field, despite the fact that by following a corn row they could reach the field edge. It was a case of panic induced by the inability to see very far.

Through August there is nothing to do but wait on the corn; the heavy work with the crop will come later. Tobacco, too, requires little work in August other than worming or topping the crop. One who walks tobacco fields this month may see the torn leaves of tobacco plants, the efforts of skunks getting the large tobacco worms they relish.

In pre-combine days, much threshing was done in August, principally threshing out of the barn. Wheat and oats were hauled to the barn and stored for later threshing; it was believed that putting the crop through a sweat would make better grain and straw. August work was devoted to hauling manure, scything weeds along fencerows and in dry pastures, and perhaps making a second cutting of hay.

In the hill country where the past is not quickly discarded, it is a common sight to see summer kitchens, usually with a springhouse attached. These buildings, vintages of the past, always look cool on hot summer days, suggesting cold spring water and other simple treats.

The Sioux called August the Ripe Moon, a time when favorite wild fruits became available. The Creek referred to August as the Big Ripening Moon. Both of these names allude to August as a time of plenty in the Indian year. Wild foods are still abundant, although few moderns make use of them. Late in the month blackhaws ripen; these rich, sweet, prune-like fruits were greatly appreciated by boys a few generations ago; they would keep secret the location of blackhaw patches.

May apples or mandrakes are ripe. These superb wild fruits are little known today; in the past they were eaten with gusto. Gathered when they are golden yellow and squeezed until the pulpy contents are liquefied, may apples are delicious. They possess a hard-to-define flavor, one which has been described as resembling grape, pineapple, or strawberry, or a blend of these. Euell Gibbons gives details for making an excellent may apple marmalade in his book, *Stalking the Wild Asparagus*. It is time that may apple virtues become more widely known.

There are other wild fruits available for eating out of hand or as the basis for making jam or jelly: wild cherries, choke cherries, elderberries, and, late in the month, wild grapes.

Nuts are full sized, and the squirrels cut industriously. Hickory nuts, walnuts, butternuts, hazelnuts, and even beechnuts are available; they offer some of the finest, most distinctive flavors of any nuts in the world. Yet they are ignored, probably because they are abundant and easy to get. Every year tons of these excellent nuts go to waste.

Some flavorful mushrooms are ready for the taking: chanterelles, oyster mushrooms, meadow mushrooms. Sheep pastures, when doused with rain, usually produce meadow mushrooms abundantly.

Milkweed pods are at the stage when they were used by the Plains Indians as food; they were boiled with buffalo meat to make one of their favored dishes.

Frog and turtle hunters get busy in August, taking these aquatic creatues, which yield gourmet-quality flesh. On still nights, the frog hunters' lights stab the bottomland darkness; their conversation carries well on the damp night air. Turtle hunters set baited lines in deep pools to take big snappers.

Perhaps the best, certainly the most abundant of wild nature's offerings, come to fullness in August. The word August means harvest!

In Europe, first-fruit festivals, called the Gule of August, were held in early August. Now gardens and orchards pour out their

wealth in abundance. Muskmelons, sweet corn, lima beans, tomatoes, and peaches delight trenchermen, as tables are loaded every day with the finest food. It is a time to can, preserve, and
store, and country kitchens throughout the land are steaming
with their spicy, sweet fragrances. Now, with home freezers,
much produce is frozen. Either way, August richness is being
preserved to be enjoyed throughout the coming year.

I have a childhood memory that has never faded—the fragrance of muskmelons on the night air in Greenville, the county
seat. During fair week, Indiana melons were brought in and sold
in streetside market stands. Their fragrance spread over the
neighborhood, and it was most noticeable at night when coolness
and dampness intensified the scent. It remains an unforgettable
essence associated with the peaceful, somnolent, pre-World War
II town on a summer's night.

A somewhat similar association occurred when I visited a city
uncle and aunt in the 1920s. They had an icebox—a great treat
to a country boy used to runny butter—where they cooled food
and drinking water. When muskmelons were cooled in the icebox, they flavored the water; this taste of melon-flavored cold
water remains a symbol of opulent city living to me, always associated with a gratuitous luxury.

As the richness of the August harvest draws to a close, all of
these bits of evidence of the month's mood come together, and
suddenly the observer becomes aware that a lovely northern
summer is coming to an end, a sad end despite the earlier dog
days discomfort.

There are many ways to capture the mood of August. A favorite way to escape dog days sultriness is to visit Lake Erie. A
large body of water always inspires a recreational attitude on the
part of the observer, more so if the observer is from the hot,
humid hinterland. Cool lake breezes, long vistas of water and
misty islands, the incessant cries of gulls and of terns floating in
the air, long lines of low flying herons trafficking between the
islands in late afternoon, utility wires laden with swallows and
martins, all are a refreshing sight to the inlander. The perfectly

timed antics of a group of sanderlings feeding at the ever-moving water's edge, their movements as liquid as the waves, is a cool, pleasant image, one that comforts and assuages the heat and humidity of the mainland.

The sight of sleek pleasure boats with their cargoes of happy passengers as well as the white canvas of graceful sailboats, sturdy fishing vessels, and the appearance of long lake-boat smoke trails on the horizon create a sense of restlessness. Shore and island residents live by ferryboat schedules; excursion boats to the islands or to Canadian ports promise a peep into a different world for the visitor.

There is special allure to the sprawling, somnolent marshes along Lake Erie, too. They are bright with pink mallow bloom in August and noisy with the mysterious voices of unseen wildlife. Purposeful waterfowl flights over the marshes and along the lakeshore add to the allure.

Stand by a large swamp or marsh as a storm is building. These wet areas, lush with vegetation, brood in the late summer sun, hiding the teeming wild creatures. At night they become noisy with weird, mysterious cries and calls, but just before a storm, these cries become deafening, especially the rollicking, unearthly barred owl calls. Humorous at other times, they now become frightening with their hysterical cackles.

At the large duck club marshes, mid-August is the time when the workers cut bluejoint grass with scythes, bundle it, and haul it to the workshop. There the grass is simmed (sewn) into blinds for the duck hunters' boats. Along the highways, signs advertise cattails for sale for the craft worker. Nowhere else in the state could these two scenes be witnessed; it is an entirely different world.

In such an atmosphere, it is not surprising that waterfowl decoys are important. Originally utilitarian in purpose, waterfowl decoys, now highly prized as early American folk art objects, are in demand by collectors. By combining a hunter's knowledge and instincts with creative ability, decoy carvers have become recognized artists, and their carvings are a popular form of art. John Sharon of Oregon, Ohio, is one of the best of these artists. He hunted waterfowl for many years in the Lake Erie marshes and began carving decoys because he says he couldn't afford to buy them. Eventually he turned to carving miniatures of waterfowl and other marsh birds. His carving of a miniature heron, a confidence bird used with waterfowl decoys, is perhaps one of his finest pieces, one which stamps him as an artist. Another Ohio decoy carver of note is Josef Wooster of Ashley. Joe also started out carving waterfowl decoys for hunters, and he, too, soon changed to carving miniatures. Wood ducks were long a favorite of his, but he won his greatest acclaim carving loons, a mysterious water bird that always fascinated Joe.

Sun or storm, there's abundant mood on and around Lake Erie. Nighttime travelers on lakeshore roads breathe deeply of the cool, damp night air, with its freight of peach and muskmelon scent dominating all the other rich fragrances of the productive, golden shore.

In the western Ohio of the past, boys of farm and village had their own special way of celebrating this fruitful time without leaving the home community. When the heavy promise of the month was at its height, they would gather "by the river" for an all-night revel in the abundance. "Going wild" it came to be known, and it commonly took place on Saturday night.

The boys would gather at some special site along the creek, one long known for good fishing and swimming, to practice outdoor skills and soak up the seasonal mood. These traditional sites usually had several features in common. There was a deep, dark pool of considerable size. Invariably there were high dry banks and a fringe of giant, splotched sycamore trees, usually roped together by giant, grappling grapevines. Often the remote spot was located near a railroad bridge, sometimes by a railroad water tower, and there was a well-beaten path leading to it. The boys instinctively chose an idyllically beautiful, secluded vale, one which bore an air of mystery, promise, and brooding silence. Its heavy use was indicated by stone-circled campfire sites and by forked sticks set in the ground to hold untended fishing poles.

Some Saturday evening, the boys would come to swim after a day in the fields. If the mood of the stream and the season were right, someone would suggest an overnight camp. The spontaneous suggestion would catch the imagination of the group and preparations would start immediately. There was little to do but get a fry pan, a coffeepot, and some coffee and salt. Once at the site, the group would divide into parties; one would set trotlines and hunt for frogs, and the other would set out on a foraging trip after roasting ears, melons, tomatoes, potatoes, apples, and whatever else was available from surrounding farms. Wood was gathered for a night of heat and light. Then the campers would swim in the warm, spermy creek water to cool and relax.

With a good fire burning, they would start the feast. Fish and frogs were fried over the campfire; potatoes and corn were cooked in the hot coals. These delicacies would be eaten by the hungry vagabonds along with creek-cooled tomatoes and sweet, musk-scented melons. The boys would then settle around the campfire with a pot of coffee for a long evening of storytelling. If the event occurred during the cool green-gold days, the fire was doubly welcome.

A layer of wood smoke would spread over the vale. The cool air was sweet with aromatic sycamore balm, especially noticeable after dew fall. Firelight flickered on the white sycamore trees. The restless murmur of the creek was drowned out by the rhythmic chorus of insect and amphibian calls close by. Now and then, these ever-present sounds would be broken by the antiphonal hooting of owls, the startled shriek of a shitepoke flying up the creek, or the noisy jostling of blackbird flocks roosting in the floodplain trees. There was solid contentment in this far-away-and-long-ago scene with figures leaning and lounging around the bonding campfire.

Much later more food would be cooked and eaten; the drowsy campers would then drift off to sleep around the fire, probably shivering under the spell of the mysterious, beckoning atmosphere. As they teetered on the edge of consciousness, they probably vowed to make a thousand more such camps. If they were lucky, they might "go wild" once or twice again in August before time and care caught up with them.

September

In September, leaf fall has begun in ten thousand American towns and villages, dropping the concentrated sunlight of summer on lawns and sidewalks. The fallen leaves swirl in the gusts of passing automobiles and scratch over sidewalks and street surfaces when September breezes blow, helping to create the mood of this month.

Leaf fall is sad because it reminds of sun and warmth and brightness, and of life gone for the year. Dead leaves always remind of what is past, even though the present is bright and pleasant. The sad and melancholy days are almost here, but the mood is a sweet sadness because of the fleeting beauty.

The month is two-thirds summer by astronomical reckoning, although the drift is toward autumn throughout the month. September is the herald of autumn; it holds the richness of summer while introducing fall elegance. The autumnal equinox occurs; days grow shorter. Late in the month, cold, slate-gray, equinoctial skies may bring rain, yet the month is traditionally dry. The celestial machinery does not vary whatever the conditions on planet earth.

Days are warm and sunny, but nights are cool. Often the morning lowlands are covered with mist, and vapor loaves form over lakes and ponds. On such nights, the air from the lowlands is heavy with organic pungence, a seasonal scent. The month delights the senses and lifts the spirit.

There is an old saying that "September slips down the river"; it must have been inspired by the sight of bright fallen leaves floating down a September stream. It has been said that the ninth month begins with the ending of summer and ends with the beginning of autumn. The trend of the season is pronounced enough to encourage the first winter preparations. The season followers, those who strongly feel the rhythm of the seasons, gratefully respond to September.

Vegetation is dying, but the landscape is highlighted by bright wildflowers. The flaming red cardinal lobelia of the wet woods is typical. Fencerows are orange-hued with bittersweet, considered by many to be the symbol of autumn. I remember seeing a sprig of bittersweet placed in the casket of an elderly woman by her son. His comment was that she had experienced a difficult life with little opportunity, but she had made the most of what came her way, and as a result her life was an example of beauty and sweetness. Bittersweet was the perfect personification.

September is the goldenrod month, with the goldenrods at their abundant best. Sumac seed heads are a satiny mahogany. Late in the month, New England asters will show their deep purple flowers; then monarch butterflies will be hovering over them. The prairies are bright with yellow bloom and bluestem purple haze; butterflyweed's stabbing orange still dots roadsides. Joe Pye weed towers above other wildflowers; magenta and yellow ironweed are fading.

In the woods, the distinctive pattern of baneberry doll-eyes holds the attention; woods asters brighten dark corners, spicebush leaves yellow, and shiny red jack-in-the-pulpit berry clusters are prominent. Colorful, wide-hatted fungi are plentiful with rain. Late in the month, witch hazel blooms and the sulphur-yellow blossoms lighten shady glens. In the hills, root diggers are active; they hurry to gather the valuable ginseng root while yellow leaves and red berries render it conspicuous. Leaf color increases and leaves start to fall. When yellow leaves cover the ground, they reflect their color upward; the woods is underlighted to give it a luminous, unreal appearance for a brief time. September smells of mortality as the leaves oxidize, molder, and disintegrate. John Muir wrote, "Nature doesn't waste. Her materials go from use to use, being constantly recycled in some form"—a comforting thought during this season of death and decay in the plant world.

September hikers pick up burrs of many kinds as they walk in the woods and fields. Along the creeks, big, leathery sycamore leaves plane to earth. Hemlock groves smell strongly of their evergreen essence on cool evenings after a hot day. This is an excellent time to hike the Buckeye Trail, a statewide hiking trail through some of the most spectacular scenery and most historic land in Ohio. There are 1,100 miles of trail, and it touches all parts of the state. September's golden weather offers near ideal hiking conditions: the time of dog days heat is past, the annoying insects are thinning, and lush summer vegetation is dying down. It is a fine time to capture the rich and varied moods of the Buckeye state.

One can start at Cincinnati, hike eastward through increasingly rougher country, past scenic lakes, through rugged state forests and remote wildlife lands. Turning northward in eastern Ohio, the hiker views strip farming in the steep land, passes through the Muskingum Conservancy District lake country, an area where much important early Ohio history was enacted, and enters the Connecticut Western Reserve region of northeastern Ohio. Here the colonial architecture of homes and churches and the grid system of highways are distinctive. At Lake Erie, the trail turns west and parallels the lake across the northern edge of the state. When the trail turns south toward Cincinnati, it again parallels historic places: the routes of the armies of St. Clair and Wayne, or of the Miami and Lake Erie canal. It also runs through some of the most productive land in the nation. Hiking the Buckeye Trail will put one in touch with the essence of Ohio.

Changing weather and changing vegetation help to trigger the main migration of birds. To the Cree, September is the Moon When Birds Fly Away, a simple statement of the sad fact of impending cold. Following the nesting and rearing season, birdcalls are incomplete, only suggestions of the full-throated ebullience of spring and early summer. Perhaps the most noticeable are the quaker-toned warblers because of their abundance during a heavy wave; the woodlands are alive with them during large migration movements as they flit and feed. Many a squirrel hunter has had his first awareness of the little birds when the trusting warblers fed within a few feet of his position at the base of a tree.

The woods are intriguing at this season. Hummingbirds are feeding at jewelweed; pewees are still uttering their plaintive calls. There is the muted whisper conversation of bluejays, interrupted occasionally by one of their ringing cries of aggression; the galloping cadence of yellow-billed cuckoo calls trails off to nothingness in the timeless setting. Flycatchers' snapping beaks reduce the insect population. I once had one of the small flycatchers snap up an insect just two feet above my head as I sat in a squirrel woods.

The hawk migration is on in September, and the woods are full of hunting hawks. I remember witnessing a red-tail after a red squirrel. The bird, perched in the top of a tall hickory, watched the squirrel for a long time. Finally, when the squirrel ventured away from the trunk onto a small limb, the hawk struck in a long dive. But the squirrel saw it coming and quickly flipped over the limb. The red-tail, apparently young and inexperienced, hit the limb hard and turned a series of somersaults before it could right itself.

Occasionally one may see a kettle of migrating hawks riding the thermals, silhouetted against the cerulean sky. A common fascination of those who spend time in the autumn woods is the behavior of red-tailed hawks. They will fly above a woods screaming shrilly, then circle to climb high in the sky. On a sunny day, as they wheel and turn, the sun may catch the glossy sheen of their underwings and send a bright flash down to the watcher. It is an inspiring sight, one suggesting wild freedom, and one which has captured the attention of many outdoor people; often those witnessing such behavior change their attitude toward birds of prey from one of enmity to an appreciation of the esthetics of the big birds. Rarely, the high-flying hawk will go into a long stoop, rushing downward at high speed, only to turn up sharply just above the treetops in a playful, smart aleck display.

In late afternoon or just before a storm, barred owls frequently begin their social conversations; their comical, antiphonal hooting bouncing around the woods brings smiles and even laughter to the listener. It's a shame James Agee never heard barred owls calling; his imaginative treatment of it would have made classic reading.

Killdeers, flying over the fields, utter their weary call, but it is abbreviated and abrupt compared to the summer song. Late migrating nighthawks flying against a late summer sky with a sliver of a new moon behind them make one aware of the season. Occasionally starling flocks may be seen feeding over cornfields, circling, diving, darting—a vortex of energy.

Goldfinches find thistle patches and gather there as thistle floss starts to blow—a bright, diagnostic scene. Lingering swallows still gather on the wires. Bluebird families flock to the lowlands where many spend the winter. One cool evening when the lowlands were covered with mist, I witnessed a sight that seemed not of this world. As I drove by a wide, mist-covered creek bottom, I saw a great horned owl perched in the top of a dead tree, which extended above the layer of dense mist. This disembodied scene might have been a surrealist painting, a dream-like perception of space, one out of touch with reality. The sight of a great horned owl, a creature completely of this earth, surrounded by clouds brought together the real and the ethereal in a striking manner, one I can never forget.

The waterfowl migration is in progress; big ducks arrive in Ohio. Creeks, ponds, and lakes harbor the feeding and resting birds. Wood ducks fly up creeks, a familiar sight. Tourist geese assemble on large bodies of water and grow restless. In waterside woods, turkey vultures still are mustering. On sunny mornings, they occupy all perching sites, even the ground where they spread their wings to dry in the warming sun. Once dry, they soar aloft to scour the land. In the evening they return, large flocks lazily circling to finally funnel down to their mustering site—a scene out of antiquity.

With the coming of cooler nights, the mammals start to get ready for winter, and the outdoors is busy. Game trails are heavy as the earthbound critters feed, store, build, or laze in the sun. The woods are noisy with the sound of falling nuts as squirrels cut acorns, hickory, beechnuts and, later, walnuts. The sounds of gnawing squirrels and the light patter of cuttings on the leafy woods floor often lull the squirrel hunter, weary from city bustle, to sleep. Red squirrels, chipmunks, and mice are busy gathering and storing. Woodchucks alternate between stuffing themselves with rich legumes and soaking up enough sunlight to last them through to spring. Muskrats start building their houses. Coons sprawl out on the high limbs of trees to soak up the sun. Shrews are rarely seen, but occasionally one will appear.

One September day, while resting near a cradle knoll on the trail through the Great Swamp in New Jersey, I watched a shrew rush out of hiding to capture and consume an insect within six feet of where I sat with my granddaughter.

White-tailed bucks polish their antlers, rubbing them on shrubs and small trees to get rid of the velvet. Fawns lose their spots but not their adolescent playfulness. Red squirrels bark their jerky alarm calls at invaders, and the tireless clucking of many chipmunks has a hypnotic effect on those in the woods. The magic time of autumn is well started.

In northeastern Ohio, I used to find jumping mice on dry, grassy sand or gravel knolls; presumably they were gathering there to hibernate away from the wet soils so common to that region of the state.

The return of beavers to Ohio has had great favorable impact; the increase in beaver ponds and swamps has resulted in more wildlife. Prothonotary warblers, formerly uncommon, have increased considerably as more wooded swamps have been created. Great blue heron rookeries are more numerous. The bird population in general has increased because of beavers, whose ponds provide ideal habitat for waterfowl and furbearers as they are usually remote and inaccessible. Wood ducks are the most common duck species utilizing beaver ponds, but all migrants rest on them. Minks and coons are the fur bearers most benefitted by this habitat. Beaver engineering has helped to counter the destructive drainage of kettlehole swamps and other wetlands in Ohio.

Added to all the other sounds of September's song are the tireless stridulations of the insect musicians. The insect songs are near their peak for the warm season, and the nightly susurration of thousands of small living creatures moving over and under and through the vegetation added to these sounds swells to a loud, nocturnal chorus, the coda to the song of summer. Crickets, grasshoppers, katydids, cicadas, and numberless, nameless other insects join in this great chorus, which no ear can completely ignore. It sounds through the night, creating an indelible impression.

There is an old saying that nothing is so dauncy as a fall cricket. Yet, every grassy field is loud with cricket trill twenty-four hours a day in September. Cool nights bring the spiders into prominence. Their dew-laden webs are the perfect embodiment of the geometry of frailty. Mosquitoes are still active in September, and the ingenious ant lion tends his trap at the base of sandstone cliffs in the hills. In a year of abundant fruit, the dangerous yellow jackets are busy, especially near a food supply. Praying mantises work the fencerows for insect prey, their flailing flight easy to identify.

Best of all is the beauty pageant of moths and butterflies visiting the tall, bright blossoms of the month. Perhaps the favorite of this fragile clan is the monarch, September's butterfly. The brief, idyllic days when monarchs seem to fill the air, dancing over goldenrod and purple New England aster are known as Monarch Days; they occur during the monarch migration when these tawny sparks of autumn cease their idle wandering and set out with purpose for the Southwest. The sight of monarchs at these autumn wildflowers is the essence of fall. I once sat by a fallow field grown to goldenrod and scattered New England asters on a late September day, listening to Schumann's Piano Concerto in A Minor while watching monarchs dancing over the field. They sought the intensely purple aster clumps where they alighted and fed; then they fluttered into the cider-sweet autumn air, danced away from the asters, and circled, only to agree and return again and again to the asters, in time it seemed, to the conversation between piano and orchestra, rising and falling with the music. Suddenly they flew across the gold and purple field—swiftly, as if caught by a freshening breeze—and disappeared. It was a rare moment, one by which to always remember the Ninth Month.

And when the monarchs migrate, can the crawling woolly worms be far behind? There is, in fact, a country saying that when the monarchs migrate, soon the woolly worms will be crawling, referring to the sight of these caterpillars crossing highways, searching for a place to spend the winter. It is an accurate phenological relationship.

Honeybees are busy making the dark honey characteristic of the late season—buckwheat, goldenrod, aster, and, best of all, according to the hill country wild bee hunters, honey made from steelweed, a wild aster. Starting in September, the wild bee hunters line bee trees for cutting when cool weather quiets the swarms and improves their disposition.

Turtles sun on logs and rocks; in the hills, reptiles move to hibernation points. Chimney swifts flock in small towns. Screech owls send their comforting, quavering calls from village cemeteries.

September was the Harvest Moon of some Indian tribes, the time of the large wild reaping. By the European formula, the Harvest Moon is the full moon nearest the autumnal equinox. This may be either September or, less commonly, October. The major harvest is done during these two months. September is the last of the tender harvest, those crops vulnerable to frost.

With cooler nights and the reminder that frost is not too far distant, those with a strong provider instinct go afield to prospect and to gather. Originally it was done by the entire family to assure plentiful food for winter. Now that man is less subject to the vagaries of nature, the provider instinct is manifested mainly by boys and men.

Sixty years ago, with the start of school in September, rural children, especially those from old-fashioned families who abided by the past, would proudly bring uncommon treats to school. It was a common practice to bring a bag of large, well-flavored red haws to be eaten behind large geography books. Children would bring beechnuts, black haws, or pawpaws they had seined from forgotten corners. Or it might be parched corn, cracklings, or other unusual food treats. Today, if it can't be purchased at a store, it won't be eaten.

There are a number of wild foods of gourmet quality available to the knowing and energetic. May apples are probably most available in September when their golden color catches the eye. Many wildlife species also eat them. Late in the month, black haws ripen. Other wild fruits and berries available include wild grapes, elderberries, wild cherries, chokecherries, wild plums, and pawpaws. These may be eaten fresh or made into jams or jellies. Red haws are made into a well-flavored, uniquely-colored jelly.

The woods are full of colorful fungi if there has been adequate rainfall. Most are poisonous, but there are excellent food mushrooms. Jerusalem artichoke, a wild sunflower, thrives in many soybean fields; they were dug by Indian squaws as an important source of food. Under the name "sun chokes," they may be purchased at a fancy price, or they may be dug by an energetic provider. To seek these unusual foods in the outdoors adds another dimension to outdoor enjoyment.

The greatest harvest from the wild through the centuries has been made by hunters. Since wild game was the major source of food, there is little wonder that the atavistic urge to hunt is strongly established in so many. One of the most idyllic forms of hunting occurs in September when squirrel hunters take to the woods. Rip Van Winkle hunted squirrels to escape his wife's scolding tongue, and the peace and beauty he found there is legendary. Ever since, hunters have taken to the woods largely to escape the cares and pressures of this demanding world; squirrel tails tacked on the woodshed have long been badges of pride and contentment. The fact that squirrel hunting occurs when the woods are near their beautiful best does nothing to detract from this popular pastime. I once heard a city man, originally from the hills, say that when he saw bittersweet twigs in the buttonholes of men's jackets, he became homesick, and he knew that only a squirrel hunt would cure it.

The squirrel hunter enters a sun-dappled woods at a time when bird migration livens the scene. Leaves are turning; the woods floor is lightened by bright berries and wide-hatted fungi. There is a languid atmosphere despite the high sense of anticipation. The hypnotic clucking of drowsy chipmunks in the peculiar acoustics of a squirrel woods sets the stage for the hunter. Often squirrel hunters are country-born individuals lured to the city by employment and away from the contact with the outdoors they knew on the farm. To these people, squirrel hunting is a way to keep in touch with the reality of the earth.

The wild harvest in any of its forms is a pleasant, valuable way to enjoy September. The stress of production is past; now is the glory of the harvest. September is the fulfillment of spring and summer promise.

When I was a boy, our farm had many rail fences, carryovers from the pioneer period. In the years following World War I, my father converted from rail fences to woven wire. This occurred when I was at the proper age to convert rails into stove wood with a bucksaw, and every Saturday morning during fall and winter I sawed rails—a highly destructive activity, as I later discovered.

The rail fences I remember best are those that bordered the woods on two sides. The east side of the woods had about one hundred rods of fence, one of the longest stretches of contiguous rail fencing I can remember. The sturdy, gray, lichen-covered, weathered fence was overhung in many places by tree limbs, which gave squirrels and coons access to the traditional wild-life highway. The top rails were worn smooth from countless scratches and claw marks of the traveling creatures—squirrels, coons, chipmunks, weasels, possums, and mice. The fence ran close to briar patches and a pawpaw thicket, and at the north end it ran near the stump pile—a giant, tangled haven for wildlife— the remains of twenty acres of woods that had been cut in 1913 to rebuild a barn destroyed by fire.

In the morning sun, the gray fence stood bold against the green bank of the woods. In the evening shadows, it was more intimate, with red streaks of sunlight striking through the woods, lending even more enchantment to the old fence. Its brush-filled angles hid many a rabbit that we jumped during family rabbit hunts. It was also a favored squirrel hunting site, and I sat on it unnumbered times to wait for fox squirrels to appear in the coppery evening sun.

Memories of that sturdy, weathered piece of pioneer agricul-tural architecture rank high. What I would give to be able to climb up on a broad top rail to wait for the appearance of a Halloween-orange fox squirrel on a big sugar tree, soaking up enough peace and contentment in the quiet eventide to last through life.

Today the major harvest of the Harvest Moon is done on the farm. Then, when the tender harvest is largely completed, the ingathering of the hardier crops is begun. Farmers welcome this season, the time of Sleepy Hollow plenty, the time when the sea-son's abundance is reckoned. It has traditionally been the time of the heaviest work, but cooler weather and the anticipation of harvest keeps it hopeful and pleasant.

Corn, which was green at the month's beginning, has browned; husks are dry by the month's end. In the hills and in Amish communities, corn is cut by hand, and the order of a field of shocked corn is comforting. Silo-filling occurs on dairy farms. Soybeans change from green to peach and finally to brown as the month progresses. By late September, gum-heavy tobacco is cut and hung in the shed to be safely housed ahead of a killing frost.

In the past, almost every farm had a patch of sorghum cane. Before a frost, the cane had to be stripped of leaves, cut, topped, and the stalks tied in bundles. It was then stored indoors until hauled to the sorghum mill, where the sweet juice was squeezed from the stalks and boiled into pungent, tasty, dark sorghum molasses. All of this work had meaning when the crocks and cans of molasses were brought home and stored for the cold months. Throughout the winter, it was spread on bread, pancakes, pumpkin pie, or on anything else that fancy dictated. This simple pleasure lent meaning to the season, with the homemade aspect giving it more significance than if the treat had been merely purchased at the store.

Another common sight throughout the summer was a yard picket fence lined with canning jars turned upside down over pickets as they were emptied and set out to air. By September they were being taken inside to be filled again with the lavishness of truck patch and orchard; the spicy sweet fragrance in country kitchens strengthened the sense of seasonal awareness even more.

The fragrance of plenty is present everywhere. From orchards come the winey scent of fermenting fallen apples. Basketed red apples and yellow peaches scent the air. Truck patches waft the fragrance of muskmelons and tomatoes. During this time, melons, sweet corn, squash and other choice vegetables are at their highly flavored best. It is a pleasant time to stand downwind from a roadside market to inhale the September breeze.

Mood increases every day. On a September day, one may arise to the golden glow of sunlit early fog; move through an active day of color, abundance, and cider-sweet air; witness a brilliant autumn sunset against a violet horizon, and go to bed by the light of a bright harvest moon. That's about enough beauty for one day. Little wonder that September is known to some as the Golden Month.

The Harvest Moon's signature is written in many ways. The green-gold days occasionally found in August become a regular occurrence this month. Almost every day is pleasure, a cooler time after hot weather, one which presages the coming of autumn and Indian Summer spells. On such days, the sun shining through the green foliage creates the green-gold atmosphere conducive to a strong sense of well-being. September is a cool, contemplative month.

There is a great unreasoning joy in the things of the earth as the growing season nears its end—appreciation for past warmth, but delight in present goodness. A falling leaf, a lichened log, a patterned stone, a familiar fall woods floor—any one of these can send an earth lover into ecstasy. John Muir stated it well when he wrote, "After a day spent in the woods, we are already immortal." The autumn woods is the best of earthly immortality. This is the time to store courage for the winter ahead, especially so in view of the world energy problem. The woods become bright with leaf color, especially on sunny days when berry-bright and nut-brown are diagnostic colors, but they can also be dark-aisled when the equinoctial gloom settles in late in the month. Leaf fall begins in September, even though the heavy fall commonly occurs the following month. While the leaves remain, a sun-dappled woods floor is a mark of the month. Season-watchers puzzle all month over when summer ends and autumn begins, and they awaken one morning to discover it is autumn, its arrival being so gradual that it was never exactly noted.

The dying season is a fairyland of shy, secret beauty as the change from summer richness to autumn elegance takes place. The woodland fifers and drummers play a tune to march by: woodcock wings whistle in the aspen, and the drumming of ruffed grouse echoes from the wooded ridges. Sycamore's healing balm floods the bottomlands. In the past, September meant school and the end of a summer of barefooted freedom as rural children laced up tight, uncomfortable shoes.

September skies vary from delicately tinted evening tones to lurid, blood-red western brilliance at sunset. Frequently the northern lights flash and dazzle, an awe-inspiring sight with which to end the front porch season. Finally the dark equinoctial storm clouds arrive, bringing the rain associated with seasonal change. There is a dreary period, but invariably it is succeeded by the wonders of October.

October

October, the Moon of Falling Leaves to eastern Indians, is a favorite time of the year for those in tune with the earth's rhythms. Ernest Thompson Seton in his book, *Rolf in the Woods*, faithfully depicts the character of a spiritual Indian in the person of Quonab. Near the end of his life, the old Indian expresses the following prayer: "Oh, God of my father, when I reach the Happy Hunting, let it be ever the Leaf Falling Moon, for that is the only perfect time."

What a touching statement of the virtues of October! The Tenth Month contains all the elements necessary for joy and happiness, as the wonder of summer lives on into the glory of autumn to bring a near perfect state of mind. But October brings both peace and restlessness; there is the peace of fulfillment of the sedentary man and, at the same time, the restlessness of the ancient provider—the hunter and forager.

Indian Summer comes most often in October. Perhaps that is why the month is appreciated by so many. A large stationary mass of warm, tropical air hovers over the northern states following Squaw Winter, a brief, cold, stormy period. This lingering air mass fosters the sense of lassitude so familiar during this enchanted time. The weather is warm and dry, the sun mellow; it is a calm month, speckled with gentle breezes. The sky is an ultimate blue, and the air, hazy as if from the smoke of legendary Indian campfires, softens and tints the distant horizon. Heat shimmer over harvest-brown fields forms a mirage. Gossamer strands of spider silk or vegetable floss float in the air, glistening in the sunlight, disappearing, then reappearing as they catch the light again. The unhurried sounds of the season add to the illusion of leisure. The quiet scene is marked by indolent insect calls (for only the insects fiddle and cry to the last), by spasmodic chipmunk clucking or, occasionally, by the haunting passage songs of migrating Canada geese. Crows caucus and beech tree foragers feed and fatten against the coming cold. Nights are cool, the stars glitter, and the orange moon is large. Helen Hunt Jackson aptly described this bewitching time in her delightful poem, "October's Bright Blue Weather":

> Oh sun and skies and clouds of June,
> And flowers of June together,
> Ye cannot rival for one hour
> October's bright blue weather.

It is Indian Summer witchcraft that no one can completely ignore.

This benevolent holding still of the season's advance touches the heart of man. It is a second chance, the blessing of warmth and beauty after it appears that cold, blustery weather has begun. This period of grace brings peace of mind and a relaxed, unhurried air, even though illusory with the benevolence being so brief.

Elegant October is the time of the chromatic feast. The chemistry of autumn brings brilliant color to the eastern woodlands, one of the brightest regions in the world for leaf color, due chiefly to abundant maples. The observant can read the composition of the woods by their color. John Burroughs wrote, "Now is the time of the illuminated woods; they have a sense of sunshine even on a cloudy day, given by the yellow foliage; every leaf glows like a tiny lamp; one walks through their lighted halls with a curious enjoyment." Woods walkers will observe that one yellow tree lights an entire woods, sending its glow into the darkest corners, releasing the sunlight the leaves fed upon all summer. Blue cohosh berries contrast pleasantly with the fallen yellow leaves. Then one may say with the poet, "If eyes were made for seeing, then beauty is its own excuse for being."

The vegetation of the state, especially the composition of the climax forests of each region, greatly influences a traveler's impressions. Each region has its own unique charm and value. Ohio is 27 percent forested, and forests are well managed and productive of timber, wildlife, and recreation. About two-thirds of the state was covered by the glaciers, and this area is level, productive land; more than one-third was unglaciated and is hilly. Generally, eastern Ohio has a sandstone base and the soil is acid; western Ohio is underlaid with limestone and is alkaline. These factors help to determine the vegetation. The original vegetation is the product of untold centuries of evolution into its final or climax state. A climax forest is one characterized by unchanging, dominant tree species when undisturbed by man. Since the coming of white men, the original vegetation has been greatly modified. With proper management, Ohio forests and woodlots are productive and diversified because of good soil and adequate water.

More than half of hilly, unglaciated southeastern Ohio's 6.5 million acres are forested, three-fourths being oak-hickory climax forest which thrives on the dry, well-drained soils. There are some mixed mesophytic and sugar maple–beech forests where there is more moisture. Leaf color here is largely yellow, highlighted by the pastel coloring of oaks. Sassafras brightens old fields with yellow-orange. Agriculture consists mostly of grazing on the steeper land with row crops on more favorable sites. Extensive state forests and the Muskingum Conservancy District lakes distinguish this region.

Glaciated northeastern Ohio is more level and contains 5.1 million acres, about one-fourth of which is forested. In this cooler, moister region, sugar maple–beech-yellow birch is the climax forest type with elm-ash–red maple swamp forest on the wetter sites. Soils are tight and poorly drained, and dairying is the main type of agriculture. Because of the abundant sugar maples, this region is the maple syrup center of the state, also the most colorful region. During the color season, the long slopes characteristic of this area are a riot of brilliant reds and yellows as far as the eye can see.

This region is in the transition life zone; it marks the transition from southern to northern plant and animal life, and contains forms of each. Thus it has a wide variety of both habitats and wildlife. The sugar maple–beech forests may have hemlock-lined gullies. Abundance and variety are characteristic of northeastern Ohio plant and animal life.

Level, glaciated northwestern Ohio, the Black Swamp region, contains 7.2 million acres; and farm woodlots make up the wooded area, which accounts for less than 10 percent of the land. The rich soil is intensively farmed. The woods are chiefly elm-ash–red maple swamp forest, hence the color units are smaller than in eastern Ohio, although the limited sugar maple–beech woods provide patches of bright color. There are fewer recreational areas in this region. Western plants and animals appear. The oak openings near Toledo are unique in this agricultural area, formerly one of the top ring-necked pheasant regions in the midwest.

Southwestern Ohio is largely glaciated, although the portion around Portsmouth is hilly and resembles southeastern Ohio. It contains 7.3 million acres and is mostly agricultural land. More than one-fourth of the land is timbered with a variety of forest types; sugar maple–beech, oak–sugar maple, and mixed oak are the major forest climax types. This region is colorful because of the sugar maple units; the hilly portion is less colorful. Western plants and animals are also found in this farm game region. Recreation areas are not common except in the southern portion.

One sunny October day, I was walking in a large woods in north central Ohio near the border of the northeastern and northwestern regions—an area containing features of both regions—when I came to a kettlehole buttonbush swamp. There were several red maples located in and bordering the swamp, each a pillar of scarlet flame, lighting its environs. Much of the root system of each maple grew above the wetness, forming islands. In one, a mink had established a den; its worn trails laced the mossy island. At the swamp edge, two big red maples had blown over, forming two cradle knolls. On these elevations, mats of partridgeberry grew, one of the few stands of this interesting plant to be found in this county, to my knowledge.

It was impossible not to sit on a log to look, to listen, to absorb with all the senses the classic signs of the holy Indian Summer spell. Old moss-covered logs in the swamp served as runways for visiting wildlife, as well as resting and preening places for wood ducks, which used the swamp in late summer and autumn. A nearby hollow log was covered with nutshell fragments, the midden of a chattering red squirrel. A giant, fat, prowling woodchuck approached the swamp, first moving swiftly, now stopping abruptly to look for danger. Fox squirrels barked, and chipmunks clucked drowsily from beech trees; crows worried an owl somewhere in the woods. The husky, squirrel-like calls of a red-bellied woodpecker grew monotonous with regularity. Aggressive robins dominated the wild fruit trees, engaging in almost constant aerial fights to drive away competition. A few late warblers gleaned tree bark; flycatchers hawked flying insects. Occasionally a monarch butterfly flew high above the trees, a laggard from the migrant millions stretching in a fluttering line from the Great Lakes to Mexico. Strands of gossamer filament glistened everywhere, evidence of tiny spider visitors from the stratosphere. The damp night air, weighting their strands, had brought them back to earth to decorate Indian Summer.

Leaf fall marks the definitive start of autumn, the hinge on which the season turns. Autumn's smell of mortality deepens as the summer sun's accumulated energy begins to decay, yet the dead leaves provide a pleasant, seasonal fragrance. Desultory cricket calls lend tranquility to the scene. Almost coincidentally with leaf fall comes first frost. This welcome event cleanses the air and kills the lush summer vegetation; rural hiking becomes less encumbered.

If September is the Goldenrod Month, October is the New England Aster Month. The aster's bright purple is a beacon that attracts lingering monarch butterflies. The fleeting sight of monarch brown against aster purple is one of the unforgettable autumnal color combinations, a haunting symbol of the brevity of being.

Autumn is a time of vividness before death, a fruitfulness before decay; it attains its most perfect state in October. As nature dies, man awakens, becomes keen, active, on the verge of discovery. It is a time of promise despite the end of plant life for the year. Man senses the challenge of the earth.

With leaf fall comes goose call from the blue October sky. Leaves and geese reach a time of decision together. Perhaps more goose-flock clamor has been heard while raking leaves than during any other task. The sight of migrating geese etched against the sky is one of the epic natural events of the North American continent. May there always be large flocks of geese to enliven October.

One of the most crowning outdoor sights I ever witnessed occurred at Munuscong Bay, south of Sault St. Marie, Michigan. We were hunting ruffed grouse and waterfowl, and our stay was at an end. We spent the last day in the duck blind; it was a raw, windy day with occasional snow squalls, and ducks and geese filled the bay as they moved in from the rough waters of Lake Superior.

The Canada geese were restless and noisy; they would lift off, circle the bay, and light down, only to take off soon again. This continued throughout the day. Late in the afternoon, however, they seemed to reach the moment of commitment. Large flocks took off, one after another, yet this time with purpose, as they headed south and flew out of sight. I saw more waterfowl that day than I'll ever see again. The scene must have resembled those of early, primitive America; it left an indelible impression of abundance.

Bird activity is high in October; most migrate, many feed frantically, all are getting ready for winter in their own way. Beech and fruit trees are noisy with the energetic, combative feeders—woodpeckers, nuthatches, robins, thrushes, crows. Turkey vultures, which have mustered by lakes and streams for more than a month, finally depart; they may be seen in southern Ohio circling and spiraling down the long ridges, riding the thermals to better hunting in warmer climes. From the azure sky, a red-tailed hawk screams repeatedly. The sound of unknown voices still comes from the autumn woods, adding to the mystique of Mother Nature.

To the harvesters, those with a strong provider instinct, October is a hoarding month. Man and the wild creatures store against the coming of winter. Not all put away surplus food; many store it in the form of layers of fat, which will carry them through the lean season. Insects provide for the next generation by depositing eggs that will hatch when food and warmth are again with us.

It is also a time to harvest beauty, and bittersweet bouquets brighten many homes. *Bittersweet*—a word for autumn! Its implications describe the feelings of those sensitive to the season's brilliant but fleeting beauty. The bright orange berries are a fitting symbol.

All the hoarders are busy stocking winter granaries. Once while squirrel hunting, I kept hearing action in a tall hickory tree. Nuts would drop for awhile, then there would be a quiet period, to be followed by another spell of dropping. Eventually I saw a chipmunk climb the towering tree until it was a mere speck on a high limb. Then came the thud of falling nuts. The sight of this diminutive mammal against the sky high in the tall, yellowing hickory created a dramatic picture. Small, energetic, determined, the tiny creature of small, cozy habitats had adapted to the large-scale dimensions of the tall hickory. It was an impressive display of courage.

Fat woodchucks waddle and roll over lush clover meadows, soaking up the sunlight and adding to their store of fat in their final weeks of activity. They will then retire to their burrows for four or five months of hibernation. Other mammals too are busy preparing for winter. Flying squirrel families frolic endlessly in the woods, gliding silently in a playful display. Deer begin their mating season. Creeks are centers of creature activity; animal sign is easy to see at the water's edge. Small mammal remains and wild cherry seeds in mammal scats reveal their food habits.

The overpowering night song of summer continues in subdued volume. During warm spells, insects and amphibians call, but the zest inspired by reproduction and summer atmospheric conditions is missing. Fish move to deeper water.

With frost and leaf fall, game fattens, fur thickens, and nuts ripen to brown maturity. Now comes the season for exploration, to prospect for game and fur. The red gods call most insistently; boys with walnut-stained hands roam the countryside with split-rail excitement, with much the same intense spirit of adventure exhibited by the Rocky Mountain fur trappers of early America.

In the past, the boys would visit community orchards to fill pockets with choice old apples, then head for the wilder stretches of woods and creeks. Along the way, trees with the largest, finest hickory nuts, walnuts, and butternuts would be sampled and noted for a later visit. Even beechnuts were eaten. We tend to underestimate the productivity of beech trees. Yet, in some provinces of France, in a productive year, the beechnut crop can be great enough to provide cooking oil for the entire province population for three or four years. Imagine the taste of food cooked in beechnut oil. We frequently buy foreign nuts at fancy prices believing they're superior to American nuts; often they have far less flavor and distinctiveness than our native nuts—something hungry boys have always known.

Usually a dog would accompany the foraging group, and his enthusiastic yipping as he chased rabbits or scented strong fur animal trails would fire the boys' imagination. To the zealous, exploring boys, such epic adventures represented America at its primeval best, little changed from the days of the mountain fur trappers. Game birds were calling; the boys might hear raucous pheasant cackle, plaintive bob-white quail covey calls, ruffed grouse drumming, or whistling woodcock wings, depending on their region of the state.

The most ancient form of harvesting is the chase. Hunting was man's earliest source of food; modern nimrods are merely yielding to an age-old atavistic urge. During October, the Hunting Moon of some Indian tribes, there is an abundance of hunting opportunities. Many of those who choose to recapture the early American affinity for the earth do so by going afield with gun and dog. Hunting during this illuminated month offers sportsmen the chance to walk the outdoors when it's at its best.

Squirrel hunting, which has provided sport for busy, harassed men since the time of Rip Van Winkle, is more challenging now than in September; the woods are more brightly colored, and the insect population has fallen. The hunter enters the woods cautiously; an air of great expectation hangs over the scene. The tracery of dew-laden spider webs sets the stage. The sun-dappled woods floor is virtually barren of vegetative cover but calicoed with fallen bright leaves. Tiny rose-berried euonymous, inconspicuous woods asters, and colorful mushrooms brighten dark corners. The woods is cool and so quiet that a falling leaf creates a noisy disturbance. Languid sounds and heady fragrances add to the mood.

The squirrel hunter sits on a log in a likely looking spot, waiting for the wonders of October to parade past him. Beech trees and wild grape tangles may be noisy with birds feeding for migration. It is the Feast Moon of the late birds. In the distance, crows worry an owl as they have done for ages. There is an odd light in the dim woods. Chipmunks are still giving their hypnotic, ventriloquial clucking so difficult to locate in the peculiar acoustics of a squirrel woods. The foliage takes on a different aspect to one scanning the treetops for sight of a squirrel; the depth and dimension of the upper story renders a new point of view, much the same as that of a bird-watcher focusing binoculars on a flitting warbler. Shining gossamer threads float in the air.

Gradually the slight sound of a squirrel cutting nuts is heard; falling nuts and the swish of a body leaping from one leafy branch to another rivets the hunter's attention. Or it may be a moving shadow on the woods floor near the hunter that catches his eye. Eventually a bright rufous-red fox squirrel appears in the autumn sun. The squirrel in the game bag satisfies an age-old tribal urge, a satisfying experience for the hunter in the October woods.

With game in the coat, tension is lessened. Now the hunter stops to gather a pocketful of sweet-meated hickory nuts from a favorite tree; he may take time to crack a few between stones. He may search for the site of a faintly remembered may apple patch. He notes a sapling on which a rutting whitetail buck has rubbed his antlers free of velvet. If there has been adequate rainfall, he may find oyster mushrooms on a dead tree or fallen log, a pleasant addition to the wild menu. He might walk to his automobile through a field of shocked corn, the peace of the season completely dominating the restlessness also present in autumn. En route he pauses along a fencerow to gather a bouquet of bittersweet.

In the hilly gray squirrel range, the hunter goes early to the deep, dark valleys where the light is still dim. Wary grays are difficult to approach; to hunt them in the shadowy early light is the secret to success. Often the hunter's first awareness of gray squirrel activity is the patter of dew on fallen leaves. As the squirrel moves on the smaller branches, it jars condensed dew loose from the leaves. The hunter views distant ridges with colorful oak leaves of russet, pale maroon, rusty orange, dusty rose, and tarnished gold, and he must be alert for timber rattlers and copperheads. If there has been a severe frost, he may feast on tasty persimmons.

Without doubt, the most idyllic form of hunting in Ohio is seeking the woodcock. The appearance of the timberdoodle belies his behavior; he is a comical-looking misfit, a chunky, short-legged bird with an extremely long bill, and he possesses big eyes, which are set high and far back in his large head. He is known as the elf of the woodlands. His nasal peent, a ground note given during courtship, is a raucous bronx cheer, perhaps a result of his damp, sinus-inducing habitat. Since he occupies organically rich woodlands, the bird is said to possess a "strong sense of humus." And yet, the woodcock inspires a highly romantic atmosphere during the beautiful spring courtship ritual. In flight, the ethereal whistling of his wings sets the mood for the elfin habitat he occupies in October.

Northeastern Ohio woodcock habitat is characterized by heavy, wet soils; the woods floor is hummocky and often covered with reindeer moss and other club mosses. Cradle knolls are frequent where pancake-rooted trees have fallen. Often woodcock are found along old dead furrows created when the marginal soil was still being farmed. The habitat is northern in character.

Northeastern Ohio country lore has it that the woodcock migration occurs during the first full moon after the beginning of October. This belief is based on another belief—that woodcock migrate mainly during bright moonlight nights. Woodcock are crepuscular creatures, always preferring dim light. When leaf fall thins the shade until light penetrates the cover, they become nervous and soon move out. Often this movement occurs during a frost, which frequently happens during a full moon—hence the legend. After this the woods are empty of all but woodcock splatter. Because good woodcock hunting is associated with early leaf fall, it might be said that it signals the start of autumn.

The best woodcock hunting is found when popple foliage is golden and thinning. Then, on a dreamy autumn day, a popple

thicket is a magical place, and the whistling flight of timberdoo-
dles enhances the witchcraft of the golden habitat. One October I
was hunting woodcock with a friend when he found a small bird
entangled in a heavy spider web woven in a strand of tall weeds.
It was a yellow-rumped warbler, and the struggling bird's plumage was covered with sticktights and wrapped in spider webbing,
an indication of the strength of the fragile-appearing filament.
When my hunting buddy gently removed the encumbrances, the
frightened bird darted away, visibly happy over the release.

There is a fascination surrounding migratory game birds and
their wanderings. It is especially strong at the sight of waterfowl,
such as ducks and geese. These birds, some of which nest in the
tundra and migrate across an entire continent—perhaps even to
another continent—possess a highly romantic attraction. The
flight of migrating geese or ducks carries heavy emotional impact; it always lifts and refreshes the spirit. The mystery of the
origin, route, and destination of the migrants stirs hunter restlessness. Duck migration is gradual, often hardly noticeable; the
migration of geese is spectacular and may occur in the space of a
few days with the passing of a cold front. A bird with such romantic appeal becomes the object of great interest, one which the
hunter desires to possess. To hold in hand a bird hatched in some
remote wilderness and en route to a tropical wintering ground
is to absorb some of its glamour. Such possession is strangely
satisfying.

But waterfowl hunting is far more than this. The hunter in-
vests his sport with even more romance than the quarry and its
habitat might justify. These lines by Frederick Peterson from his
poem "Wild Geese" express the waterfowler's sentiments.

> How oft against the sunset sky or moon
> We watched the moving zigzag of spread wings
> In unforgotten autumns gone too soon,
> In unforgotten springs!

Black ducks are the wariest of ducks. These large, chocolate-
brown creatures inhabit the swamps and marshes of northern
Ohio. I have watched them settle noiselessly into a dense buttonbush swamp or a sluggish, brushy stream, both favorite coverts.
Pymatuning Creek in Ashtabula County is a slow moving stream

that flows through remote, inaccessible swamps during much of
its course, and it is ideal black duck habitat. One hunt along this
wild creek remains indelibly imprinted in memory.

On a bright October day, I walked Pymatuning Creek, hoping
to jump ducks. Jump shooting along this creek is difficult. It is
necessary to quietly detour around dense thickets of swampy
dogwoods and alder, yet always be in a position to shoot when
ducks flush. The bottomland was bright with swamp holly. The
dark, placid pools were dotted with colorful floating leaves, and
the swamp maples were flaming. Suddenly six black ducks
jumped from a sheltered pool and climbed frantically to clear the
trees. Against the flaming scarlet foliage, their dark bodies made
a brief, undying picture. I snapped two quick shots and made a
lucky double on them under highly esthetic circumstances. The
beauty of the habitat and the wild energy of the climbing ducks
combined to create a permanent mental image. I had successfully
bagged two of the wariest of ducks in a scene of striking beauty,
and the combination lent a deeper dimension to the experience
than mere observation would have provided. Never imagine that
hunters go afield blind to the beauties of nature; the background
of the hunt is the element that remains longest in memory.

I remember other duck hunts made in the Moon of Falling
Leaves, for the setting and the season are theatrical and remain
in memory. I recall lying in a wet northeastern Ohio buckwheat
field at dawn, covered with straw, waiting for ducks to come to
feed. I can't remember if I bagged any ducks, but I will never
forget hearing the small sunrise sounds from a distant dairy
farm as work started for the day, nor the deep, organ-noted great
horned owl calling a farewell to the fading night.

I remember walking Big Walnut Creek in Morrow County
late one afternoon. A family of barred owls was calling antiphonally from the valley slopes, and their boisterous, jovial calls
bounced from woods to woods in the sunset. A distant flock of
wood ducks flew down the valley, silhouetted against the sunset.
From the bottomland, a pheasant cackled, a call as gaudy as his
plumage. And I'll never forget sitting in a buttonbush swamp,
surrounded by the pleasant blend of tans and greens of the
swamp vegetation, while listening to the noisy chatter of a large
flock of blackbirds. Again, I can't remember my hunting success,
but I stored memories that will last me through life. And

without the adrenalin hunting stimulates, the memories would be much less vivid. Whenever I return from a duck hunt, I recall the line from Alfred Lord Tennyson's "The Brook," "I come from haunts of coot and hern."

Hunting ruffed grouse is not at its best until after leaf fall, but the impulse to hunt them leads many to go afield earlier. On golden October days, grouse drum on distant, hazy ridges in the hills, or they may wander from dense cover to woods edges seeking food. Often they are found near wild grape tangles or black haw thickets. Ruffed grouse have increased in Ohio during the last fifty years, due largely to land use changes favorable to their needs. Statewide, there is more land in woods and brush, and grouse have increased accordingly, again emphasizing the importance of proper land use. Good habitat means more wildlife—a factor that applies to deer and other forest game.

But in spite of the handicap of dense vegetation, I recall one of my most memorable grouse hunts in an October aspen grove. My hunting companion was an elderly outdoorsman who knew the northeastern Ohio habitat well. We hunted the woods borders where aspen pioneered the way for woods expansion. After a long hunt, we finally flushed a single grouse. When I shot, the bird, which was speeding through the cover in a graceful, curving flight, suddenly began a weird, winged dance, repeatedly rising four or five feet, falling the same distance, then thrusting itself upward again in an unnatural display. Finally it collapsed and fell on the yellow aspen leaf carpet.

"It was head shot," said Charlie. "I've seen them behave that way before."

True enough, it had been head shot, one pellet hitting the bird's brain and strangely altering its flying behavior. The sight of that grouse's winged aerial dance in that golden popple setting created another mystical October image, one so typical of the bewitching season.

Charlie Searls, expert woodsman that he was, must have been possessed of serendipity; uncommon events in the outdoors were always happening in his presence. Much of this must have been due to the great amount of time he spent in the outdoors hunting, trapping, fishing, digging medicinal plants, and studying nature. I am always reminded of a small basket on their mantle, almost filled with wishbones from game birds he had taken. The man's appreciation of the outdoors equalled that of the Indians, who always practiced complete usage of anything taken from nature. The Indians were said to utter a prayer when they killed game, asking the creature's forgiveness for taking its life to sustain their own. I'd be willing to bet that if one could have read Charlie's mind, he, too, would have been conversing with the spirit of the slain creature. That basket of wishbones was heavy with meaning.

Much northern Ohio grouse hunting is done in the bright sugar maple woods, often against a dark hemlock background, and the liquid, silver notes of white-throated sparrows often fill the air. I recall another grouse hunt that must rank high among such adventures. Dr. L. D. Whitwood, a Jefferson, Ohio, veterinarian, was an expert grouse and woodcock hunter, and he kept top-notch bird dogs. Each autumn, Horace Lytle, gundog editor for *Sports Afield* magazine, came to Ashtabula County to hunt grouse and woodcock with Whitwood, and I often accompanied them. One crisp, late October day we hunted Grand River grouse covers. The river runs through high banks in this area, and its tributaries flow through hemlock-lined steep valleys. Here grouse seek hemlocks for winter cover.

On this memorable day, we hunted this beautiful habitat and flushed sixty grouse, an unheard-of success. When the grouse rose, they would fly down the valleys, swerving off laterally. I recall seeing five grouse, probably a family, flying down one of these tributary valleys and sailing up a dense, hemlock-grown lateral draw; it was a magnificent sight. Most Ohio grouse are of the red color phase, but one taken that day was a thirty-ounce, gray-tailed bird. Lytle wrote a vivid account of that hunt: The Gray-tailed Grouse. More grouse were jumped that day than I have ever again experienced or heard of in a single day's hunt. Grouse hunters of that region frequently save the tails and mount them spread fan-wise on varnished, grained wood plaques.

In my experience, October is memorable for startling outdoor scenes. One afternoon I was sitting along a country road in western Geauga County. Forest Tuttle, the Geauga County game protector, and I had just finished inspecting an area we were considering for a wildlife refuge; we were comparing notes when one of the most brilliant images ever left to me appeared. From around a bend in the road ahead of us came a group from a nearby hunt club. The master of the hunt, wearing a red jacket, was followed by members of the club, dressed in black jackets and white shirts and wearing derby hats. The contrast of black and white set against the sunny, chromatic scene was startlingly beautiful. The hunters were mounted on sleek, shining horses and were surrounded by a pack of black- and tan-spotted white foxhounds. This lively, exciting group pictured against the colorful, sunlit autumn woods created an idyllic image that I can never forget. The elegant hunting costumes, the shining, prancing horses, and the alert, energetic pack of foxhounds formed a scene of which dreams are made. They were riding toward hunting lands where they had hopes of starting a red fox.

In the hills, hunters of another kind, the ginseng seekers, spend long, silent days in the woods, looking for the yellow leaves and red berries that distinguish this valuable medicinal plant. At this time it is easy to spot, but the harvest time is brief before frost destroys the telltale leaves and berries. Sangers, a proud, traditional race, walk the sun-dappled woods with mattock and sack, watching for rattlers and copperheads as well as ginseng as they wander, stopping to feed on nature's bounty when hungry.

Lake Erie is dotted with boats of perch anglers in October, working to fill freezers for winter. Between bites they watch skeins of herons trafficking between islands. Tardy migrant swallows and martins still line utility wires. The bright lake waters are heavy with mood at this season. Inland, trotliners row to their trotlines at dawn on fog-shrouded rivers to take big shovelhead catfish during the fall feeding spree.

There is a restlessness in the Traveling or Hunting Moon, the time when the provider instinct asserts itself most strongly. Modern man has refined this instinct by making it a purely esthetic one. It is significant that hunting literature is found in the Fine Arts section of large libraries.

October was the Harvest Moon of some Indians. By European reckoning, the Harvest Moon was the month with the full moon nearest the autumnal equinox; the following month was the Hunting Moon. During the Indians' Harvest Moon, the ripeness of the year comes to reckoning, with Sleepy Hollow plenty as wild and tended bounty peaks, and harvesting becomes frantic. Farm, orchard, and garden pour out the lavish plenty from their provident cornucopias. Musky wild grapes hang heavy, and nut trees are loaded. At this time of the year, honeybees are making honey from manna or honeydew. Clem Walls, a Pike County bee hunter, said that honeydew falls from the sky during this month and lands on ash and hickory trees in the hills above the fog. "You never find it below the fog. You don't because the fog disappears it," Clem stated. The honeydew he spoke of is apparently similar to the manna mentioned in the Bible, a dried exudation of the manna ash, a tree found in the Mediterranean region. The honeydew makes the best honey there is, save maybe for steel-weed honey, according to Clem. The memory of Clem relating this arcane hill country lore always adds a special dimension to the autumn outdoors.

Farms are face-lifted by frost and the hastening ingathering. In times long gone, the harvest was a prolonged effort by hand and horse. There was always a sense of measured progress as a field was slowly harvested day by day; modern high-speed machine harvesting has destroyed much of this phenomenon. And modern agricultural methods have robbed us of the sight of a wagonload of ear-corn yellow. Gone, too, is the sight of a field of shocked corn with the shock tepees in orderly arrangement in the garnered field. Much of the esthetics of early agriculture is missing today.

October is apple time. Most apples are picked this month before heavy frost; the bright reds, yellows, and greens of the freshly picked fruit highlight roadside markets. Cider is the drink of the month. Trips to buy cider and apples are an October ritual in many families. It has been said that October is the time when juice-heavy apples have a mouth-cleansing tang they will never have again. Apples lend a special element to October plenty.

Modern taste in apples is limited to relatively few varieties favored by orchardists. It wasn't always so; in times long gone when most households had an orchard or a few yard trees, a large number of apple varieties were grown, and great pride was taken in favorite old apple trees, which yielded their goodness year after year. Then October was honestly known as apple time. Walking through an orchard bending with abundance lent a sense of infinite plenty to youths of the past. The old apples were juicy and tasty, offering a wide selection of flavors and quality. Applesauce made from an assortment of apple varieties has a flavor rarely known today; it was often called applesauce nectar. The Northern Spy was perhaps the favorite old apple. Other old favorites include Rambo, Sheepnose, Pippin, Wolf River, Baldwin, Maidenblush, Russet, Topyhocken, McIntosh, Rhode Island Greening, and Grimes Golden.

Garden and truck patch are yielding the final offerings of the year. When severe frost warnings are announced, there is a busy day of gathering the remaining vegetables and fruit and hurrying them into shelter. Then, for several days, kitchens will be rich with sweet, spicy aromas as homemakers cook and can. A favored late season product of ragged-looking gardens was last-of-the-garden relish, a delicious, pickled relish made from garden remnants. Sadly, this sense of providence is disappearing. What will children of the future have to remember of getting ready for winter, of seasonal instinct?

Anticipating the wonders, beauties, and bounties of October is exciting; the realization overwhelming. The heady scents, languid sounds, bright, retina-stimulating sights, the finest tastes of the year, the soft, tactile delights—all of these are October's gifts to the appreciative. It is "a season of mists and mellow fruitfulness," according to Keats. It is a crisp, crackling month, too, yet one of benevolent softness, a time of the procession of the many emblems of autumn.

This season of age-old signs of dying is a favorite of many because of the multitude of idyllic experiences that occur; when they are recalled, they enable one to transcend time, to relive the pleasant states of the past, for October is especially rich in association. Here are some slightly paraphrased lines from Turgenev's *Annals of a Sportsman:*

How fair is the forest in late autumn, when the snipe are on the wing. . . . You breathe tranquilly; but there is a strange tremor in the soul. You walk along the forest's edge, look after your dog, and meanwhile loved forms, loved faces dead and living come to your mind; long slumbering impressions unexpectedly awaken; the fancy darts off and soars like a bird; and all moves clearly and stands before your eyes. The heart at one time throbs and beats passionately forward; at another it is drowned beyond recall in memories. Your whole life, as it were, unrolls lightly and rapidly before you; a man at such times possesses all his past, all his feeling and his powers—all his soul; and there is nothing to hinder him—no sun, no wind, no sound.

The golden peace of the Moon of Falling Leaves is a time of sorrows healed. Spring's pleasure is one of abundant choice; autumn is acceptance of what has been given, and in this acceptance may lie the secret of contentment.

The sights, sounds, and scents of October are a continuing coda to summer's vigorous song, a time to celebrate the inexorable passage of time. Dylan Thomas, the passionate Welsh poet, wrote these lines at the death of his father: "Do not go gentle into that good night." This spirit of celebrating the death of a loved one should dictate our behavior at the passing of a beloved season; we should celebrate the passing of this dreamy, golden season with joy, each of us in our own way—naturalist or sportsman.

With the passing of the benevolent time, now comes the dark, slate-gray clouds, foretelling that the kind weather is at an end. The woods will soon be dark-aisled as winter approaches. With shorter days, longer nights, and colder weather, man will become more hearth-oriented; woodsmoke will scent the night winds, and corded stove wood will be a common sight around homes getting ready for winter.

This is the traditional time for seeking folk signs foretelling the severity of the coming sleep; the thickness of corn husks, the fatness and color of hickory nut hulls, the heaviness of goose bones, the color of woolly worms, the height and shape of muskrat houses, the location of hornet nests—all are consulted to pass judgment on the nature of the coming winter. But while the pleasant witchery of October remains, we should enjoy every enchanting moment of it.

Many years ago as a college freshman, I read A. A. Milne's essay "A Word for Autumn." Even then I appreciated his feeling for the season. Milne wrote that when the waiter put celery on the table with the cheese, he knew that summer was indeed dead; the celery marked the end of the season. This essay was written at a time when perishable foods appeared only in their season; modern agriculture and merchandising have changed all of this. Nonetheless, well-flavored celery is still a mark of the crisp time of the year, and I always associate it with autumn, especially October, thanks to A. A. Milne.

With cooler weather, the dramatic sunsets arrive, the most theatrical of the year. Appropriately, autumn is the sunset of the seasons; after it comes the long, latent sleep of winter. Autumn in American villages of the past was so beautiful it wrings the heart to think of it. On late October afternoons, boys played football in vacant lots, shouting imperatively. Small boys bantered in mimic from huge leaf piles, stuffing their clothes with leaves to simulate football padding and roughing up their play. Girls were spinning glistening batons in the afternoon sun. There was pleasant leaf smoke fragrance in the air and the leisurely labor of aproned housewives raking leaves. Aromatic smoke from leaf fires layered as it drifted down the street. A delivery truck sped by in a flurry of leaves.

The call of Canada geese came from the north. Shifting uncertainly, they tacked over the village and passed immediately overhead, calling clamorously. All eyes gazed up in awe and wonder; the watchers stirred restively as if they too should heed instinctive urgings rather than complacent duty patterns. The long, outstretched necks, the square, broad behinds, and the slow, certain wings of the migrating geese were outlined against the flawless blue sky. For a brief minute their calls stung the watchers' hearing, their flight the villagers' consciousness, and they were gone for another year. Eternal, commonplace, yet a high point of the year.

November

When Indian Summer persists into November, it is doubly appreciated. Squaw Winter has passed, and the permanent arrival of the long, cold winter is momentarily expected. The Chippewa or Ojibway of the upper Great Lakes masked their dread of the approaching cold season with a beautiful legend. Because of this late Indian Summer spell, they called November the Moon of Michabo. Michabo was their Great Spirit, and Indian Summer was a gift, a second brief summer. It was a soft name for a gentle, benevolent period; it was a second chance.

The attitude and the legend were products of centuries of difficult survival. Yet the Indians were fanciful; they fashioned something beautiful and timeless out of the harsh reality, as the name suggests. This moon name bestowed by the wistful Indians touches the heart more than most others; it has captured fancy more through the years. Even today, many individuals escape modern harsh reality in the dream world of Indian Summer.

The large stationary mass of warm, tropical air that bathes the Great Lakes region is doubly enchanting when it lingers late. Bright fallen leaves rustle to the step; a few colorful leaves still cling to the trees. But it is not fact but flights of fancy that lend Indian Summer its greatest charm! The arrival of late Indian Summer always calls to mind a cartoon in which an old man and a small boy are sitting under a tree in late afternoon. There is a field of shocked corn across a rail fence. They have been raking leaves and a leaf fire burns. The old man is conjuring the strong atmosphere of the season. He tells the boy that all homesick

"Injun" spirits come back to play where they used to live. The hazy mist, he says, is the Injun spirits dancing in the sunlight. The corn shocks are really Injun tepees, and the smoky smell in the air comes from their campfires. "Some folks say it's leaf smoke you smell, but it is really campfire smoke and the Injuns are hoppin' round them." The next picture shows the pair watching the smoke and the cornfield at dusk. A full moon is coming up behind the field, and by now the boy's imagination has converted the corn shocks to tepees and the smoky haze to misty figures of Indians dancing in the dusk.

November is a half-and-half month, a period of transition. Early November is frequently of Indian Summer benevolence, a continuation of October's elegance. The benevolence of Michabo is usually gone in the last half of the month, and commonly by Thanksgiving severe weather has set in. Scudding storm clouds bring a litany of rain to introduce the change. Often the first snowfall occurs, the cold winds blow, and streams may begin to freeze. Then the "wailing winds, and naked woods, and meadows brown and sere" of William Cullen Bryant's "The Death of the Flowers" are here to stay. The sun, giver of warmth and light, slowly withdraws its gifts. It is the beginning of hearth time. Even the most outdoor-minded individual becomes hearth-oriented when Indian Summer is gone. The transition from autumn to winter lacks the charm of the change from summer to autumn.

The brightness of chromatic October is gone, but there is still color; November has unique contributions for spirit-lifting memories. The hungry eye feasts on purple distances and pastel-shaded landscapes. The subdued beauty of oak ridges seen through autumnal haze offers a richly textured fabric suggestive of the Hudson River school, romanticized landscapes so evocative of feeling. Woods are deeply banked in fallen leaves, which are still a bright tannin brown. These insulate the ground against severe cold. Frost has killed the delicate scents; only the strong, masculine ones survive, those of harvest wealth and organic decay. Sumac and dogwood leaves, hoary black raspberry vines, and sulphur-yellow witch hazel bloom add to the modest November shading. Rose-pink wahoo leaves and hulls add a distinctive touch to the woods flavor.

Usually a few wildflower blooms have survived in sheltered sites—New England aster, black-eyed Susan, and, in damp spots, violets and dandelions. Rarely a few monarch butterflies may linger over the blossoms. Scarlet swamp holly berries highlight the bottomlands. The woods have assumed the rose-gray tone of winter. Gray, fat-trunked beech trees stand out in the bare woods.

Large flocks of thieving, nervous blackbirds traffic over fields and wetlands, uncertain as to their departure. The raucous cackle of a cock pheasant will flush them precipitously from a cornfield. In a good beechnut year, the beech trees are still noisy with the sociability of many species of feeding birds. Large numbers of woodpeckers are always present. With leaf fall, trusting pileated woodpeckers are highly visible as they perform their architectural chiseling in the barren woods. Marsh hawks fly low over brown winter fields. Kestrels are locating on utility wires near a winter food supply. In the lowlands, bluebird families sing their soft, warbling notes on warmer days, and from streamside thickets comes the liquid, silver notes of white-throated sparrows.

The winter birds arrive. The appearance of juncoes and tree sparrows is said to presage the arrival of snow. And in a year of northern migrants, pine siskins, crossbills, redpolls, snow buntings, and evening grosbeaks appear. Many share the winter feeding station with the staying species. For winter, birds are grouped, not paired as in spring. The hawks, which will winter here, are establishing themselves in good hunting territory.

Game bird calls liven November. In addition to ring-necked pheasants, the prairie roosting circle of bobwhite quail (outlined by white droppings) may be found in good cover, and at evening the plaintive, querulous covey call of a scattered flock is heard as they attempt to reassemble against the cold and dangers of the coming night; it is a beautifully touching social plea. The throbbing drum of ruffed grouse cocks sounds through the November forests, a sound which lures many to walk the paths at this time. Grouse are growing snowshoes, their special adaptation for winter. And rarely, in intimate aspen coverts, the whistling wings of tardy migrant woodcock sound.

The late migrating ducks are present, staying until more severe weather drives all but the hardiest further south. Canada geese, some of which have become year-round residents because of waste corn in mechanically picked fields, and because of successful Ohio Division of Wildlife captive goose flock management, animate lakes and ponds.

One cloudy day many years ago when I was setting a line of muskrat traps, I heard one of the greatest tundra swan flights I have ever known. The clouds were so low that day that I couldn't see the great white birds, but their soft, musical calls came down in great volume for much of the day. How magnificent it would have been to witness this gigantic movement of these splendid birds on a sunny day, when their glistening white forms, rosy in the sun, would have been outlined against a blue sky.

November was the Mad Moon of eastern Indian tribes. It was so named because then buck deer are rutting; they snort, whistle, and finish polishing the velvet from their antlers against shrubs or small trees. The peak of rutting season occurs about November 1, and occasionally fighting bucks will lock antlers and die a lingering death. The accidental highway deer kill is at its yearly peak now when deer movement is greatest. This month was also the Beaver Moon of northern Indian tribes, the time when they began to hunt beavers for food and fur.

With greater visibility in the woods brought about by leaf fall, the movements of mammals are more easily observed. The squirrel moves like a shadow through the trees or over the forest floor with a deceptive, liquid motion that earned him the name "Shadow-tail." Mink are occasionally seen bobbing lithely along a stream. The lumbering gait of a raccoon is a mixture of a trot and a canter. Those fortunate enough to observe a moving fox will witness delicate caution in action.

When a carpet of newly fallen dry leaves covers the ground, wildlife sounds are amplified, although a listener can rarely identify the maker of a tread by the sound. I flushed a woodcock in the New Lyme Wildlife Area in Ashtabula County one November day. I stopped to make a few notes when I heard the loud sound of some creature walking in the woods. I waited. I could easily have guessed that a large, heavy creature was approaching, judging from the sound. Finally the very woodcock I had flushed appeared, walking noisily through the fallen leaves.

Chipmunks are still uttering their endless, ventriloquial clucking call, and red squirrels continue to decorate trees near their home den with colorful food caches. One November day while walking through an abandoned field grown to wild apple and hawthorn, I found an old bird nest that had been remodeled. The nest had been roofed, lined, and enlarged to provide a warm, relatively safe refuge from weather and enemies. I tapped on the nest and a tawny, big-eyed deer mouse scurried out and ran along the thorny branch, stopping to peer timidly at me. I left at once and observed from a distance that the mouse returned to the nest when no longer disturbed.

The unexpected can happen in November. I was walking a fencerow when a woodchuck came running on the other side of the fence. I assumed that woodchucks were in hibernation by this time, yet this one was racing around as if it were midsummer. Another time I was prospecting a central Ohio creek when I saw a large, dark mink playing in a drift pile. It may have been hunting mice; its movements were so swift that for a moment I wondered if I was actually watching two minks. I finally made a squeaking noise; this caused the mammal to freeze, and I had a good look at him. Minks spend much more time hunting on land than is commonly known.

The winter feeding of wildlife should be started in November. Feed not only by your window; carry feed, preferably ear corn, to the thickets and lowlands where wildlife moves to escape snow and cold.

Back in the days when corn was shucked by hand, every conscientious farmer's goal was to have the corn crop in the crib by Thanksgiving. The only exception was a few shocks left to be husked on warm winter days. The sight of a lone husker at work, tossing ears in a yellow arc to the corn pile, is a nostalgic one. Usually there was a month of shucking corn on the stalk under a variety of weather conditions. Shucking standing corn is difficult, demanding labor, doubly so if the corn is broken over and repeated stooping is required. Backs ache from bending, and hands become sore and cracked from pulling back the husks and breaking off the ear. It was a common practice to carry a shotgun in the wagon to shoot the occasional rabbit seen. Often a wedge of migrating ducks would pass overhead, flying south from Grand Lake St. Marys. The tired shuckers would have to shovel the corn into the crib at noon and again at night—extremely tiring work at any time, doubly so for a weary man.

Once the standing corn was shucked and in the crib, the farmer worked at healing his sore, cracked hands. One of the common sights during and immediately after corn shucking was that of a man in his "comfort circle." The chair where he rested and recovered was located near a light, and within that circle of light was found a radio and radio log book, the daily paper, and magazines. Most important of all were the bottles of healing lotions with which he tried to heal his raw, crippled hands. Everything within this circle was there to help restore the man so he could face the work and the weather tomorrow, both of which awaited him just outside his door. When he finished shucking corn by Thanksgiving, he was doubly thankful.

With harvest completed, it was time to finish getting ready for winter. Wood was cut and ricked, hogs were butchered, and house and barn were banked to protect against the cold winds of winter in addition to other preparations. Today, growing artificiality of our existence has rendered the old traditions obsolete; getting ready for winter involves little more than resetting the thermostat. But with this greater ease of living, there has been a loss of the sense of the earth's seasonal rhythms.

November's farm colors are more subdued, but there remains pumpkin orange, squash pastel, corn yellow, fodder buff, winter wheat emerald, sky blue, and sun gold—all rich late autumn colors. Roadside markets are still bright with produce. Furthermore, the wild harvest is just coming into its own. There are still some wild fruits available, such as persimmons, wild apples, prune-like black haws, wild grapes, and red haws, and some excellent mushrooms—slippery jacks, oyster mushrooms, and late puffballs—can still be found. But the greatest wild harvest in November is made by hunters and trappers. Then Orion, the Hunter, stalks the sky, a timely appearance of this constellation when hunting activity is at its peak for the year.

For many years, upland game hunting began on November 15. The first day of rabbit season, as it was commonly called, was an important date on the calendar for many families in a slower-paced past. Boys of sixty years ago experienced a severe attack of opening-day fever. Tension had been building as the frosty, golden days of autumn sped by. Local coverts were thoroughly scouted by young hunters, usually accompanied by a dog. Never were boys and dogs any closer than during this feverish activity. Guns were polished and cleaned. Hunting was the dominant topic of conversation. Trapping season opened on the same day, so trap preparation and preseason scouting for fur sign helped to ease the unbearable buildup of tension.

On the morning of November 15, boys were up before daybreak, running a trapline by lantern light. Then they would hurry through chores and breakfast. Finally the great moment was at hand. The young hunters usually played hooky on opening day; the chase was what really mattered. The hunting party of father and sons started across the frosty fields on an unforgettable morning. The community atmosphere was usually tinged with skunk scent by then, a fragrance to young trappers, an offense to most adults.

Suddenly the idyllic scene was electric with action as a rabbit jumped from its nest and bounded away through the pumpkindotted, corn-shocked field. When the shot rang out, the rabbit rolled in the frost-covered vegetation, sending up a shower of glittering frost spangles. Sounds of the shot rolled across the frosty meadows, hit a wall of woods, and rebounded to create a confusion of echoes. The hunters' long shadows cast by the red early sun, the excited yelping dog, and the figures of other distant hunters all combined to create a Currier and Ives image that the boys could never forget.

Anti-hunters protest that hunting is cruel, yet they often overlook the suffering of gelded livestock, the dehorning of cattle, and some slaughterhouse practices. There was no cruelty or brutality in the hunting rite; it was the pure reenactment of an ancient act deeply imbedded in the tribal memory, the source of much of the enjoyment. The image of an eager schoolboy hunter or trapper is an undying one. The late Aldo Leopold, father of modern wildlife management, maintained that hunting is valuable to society for its split-rail value; boys who hunt relive the history of the nation and of the race, and the experience gives them greater appreciation of the land and the people. Leopold strongly believed that hunting was a positive value in the life of a boy.

Yet if once we efface the joys of the chase
From the land, and out-root the stud,
Goodbye to the Anglo-Saxon Race!
Farewell to the Norman Blood!

This passionate statement of the importance of hunting, not only to the individual but to a race and to national survival, was taken from the poem "Ye Wearie Wayfarer," written by Australian poet and outdoorsman A. L. Gordon. These lines appear on the cover page of *The Chase*, a magazine published for the fox-chasing fraternity, to reflect on its belief that the sport of chasing foxes is purely for the esthetic pleasure of listening to the thrilling cry of a pack of hounds. However, it stands as a justification for all hunting and its importance to a vigorous strain of men who have contributed much to the exploration and development of our planet. The poet expressed the raw fact that hunting is a sport essential to the survival of a primitive, archetypal spirit in humans. It forcefully states that the prolonged sublimation of this basic drive will endanger the essential human spirit.

Those who oppose hunting should recognize that it is another way of enjoying the outdoors. "While the earth remaineth, seed-time and harvest, and cold and heat, and summer and winter, and day and night shall not cease" is the Biblical way of describing the seasonal cycle. Also in Genesis, God tells newly created man that He has given to him every plant yielding seed and fruit, and every beast of the earth, and every bird of the air for food.

The cottontail rabbit provides more sport than any other single game species, perhaps more than all other game species combined. Most boys got their start and their early enthusiasm hunting rabbits. Real dyed-in-the-wool sportsmen never become too sophisticated for rabbit hunting.

Rabbits are basic in the wildlife food chain. Weak and defenseless except for speed and dodging ability, they are relentlessly hunted by every predator. Yet they survive and prosper in numbers because they are extremely prolific, highly cover-conscious, and very adaptable. Thus, it seems appropriate to give recognition to the lowly cottontail rabbit by enacting an Ode to the Cottontail.

Odes were originally lyric poems of praise sung and danced by Greek choruses at public celebrations. When millions of hunters take to the November fields in pursuit of rabbits, it seems proper to glorify the virtues of this legendary mammal. The high ceremony of preparing for the hunt, the act of hunting, and the hunters' lyric praise of the cottontail constitute an appropriate ode.

Cottontails weigh about $2\frac{1}{2}$ pounds. They have long, strong hind legs and powerful back muscles, which enable them to run with bounding speed. They occupy a small, cozy home range of about one acre. Within this range, there is sure to be good cover, which enables some of them to escape their many enemies. The way to have more rabbits is to provide more cover. The more briar patches, the more rabbits we will have.

Rabbits not only provide excellent, challenging sport; they are excellent on the table. Their small frame is packed with solid, sweet, well-flavored meat. The cottontail rabbit has provided countless holiday dinners to Americans through the generations. Many years ago, my son and I visited the Northern Cheyenne Indian Reservation at Lame Deer, Montana. There we met the Grooms brothers, who sold and erected windmills to provide water to this dry land. They were originally from Nashua, Iowa, home of the Little Brown Church in the Vale of hymnbook fame. They expressed regret that cottontail rabbits were so scarce in Montana. "When we were boys in Iowa, we enjoyed fried rabbit more than any other game. We could trade a piece of sweet-meated fried rabbit to children of non-hunting families at school for hickory nut cake or candy or anything else they had in their dinner pails," the brothers related with deep nostalgia. "It was the most popular meat in the neighborhood." This testimony by these two outdoorsmen speaks well for the quality of cottontail flesh, and of their value as game animals.

Late November is deer hunting season in Ohio. It is a popular pastime; red-shirted hunters are a highly conspicuous part of the landscape for one week. Ohio deer are large, fat, and well-flavored, providing a popular game meat. They also carry large antlers as long as the herd is healthy and kept within the limits the habitat will support. Ohio white-tailed deer are well represented in the North American Big Game Record Book of the Boone and Crockett Club because of the relatively small herd size and the properly managed legal kill. Ohio's Big Buck Club has done much to increase appreciation of Ohio deer. The annual Big Buck awards dinner attracts as many as one thousand enthusiastic sportsmen, who come to view what must be one of the largest displays of trophy buck heads in North America. Aldo Leopold wrote that a mountain could be damaged as severely by too many deer as a deer herd could be damaged by too large a wolf population. Wildlife must be kept in balance with its habitat. Regulated hunting is a socially desirable way of doing this.

Trapping is frowned upon by some who regard it as a cruel and useless outdoor pastime. Such critics ignore the historic role of trapping in America. Trappers were among the first to explore the North American continent and help to make it safe for settlement—a questionable achievement, according to some cultural geographers who tend to favor native populations. Once the land was settled, trappers and hunters protected crops, livestock, and even human life from excessive wildlife depredations. Even today, wildlife can become destructive if not controlled. A few years without such control can result in severe damage to farm crops. During World War II when trappers were scarce, many mammals became too plentiful and damaged crops; many became diseased, a common occurrence with overpopulation, and farmers asked for help in controlling nuisance wildlife, as they did in pioneer times. Trappers are useful to society.

To be a successful trapper, one must know the intimate habits of fur bearers and skillfully set his traps to take them. He must know weather, the habitat, and be an expert ecologist. I'll never forget the first mink I caught. One morning I walked to the creek across a field covered with the first snowfall of the season. As I approached the nearest trap, I saw movement. Struggling in the trap was a dark, beautiful mink. When I drew near, it increased its efforts to be free, its eyes emitting defiant gleams of rage. It had been caught late in the night and was still energetic in fighting restraint. My joy at catching a prized furbearer didn't prevent me from observing the creature's inability to accept its capture, its untiring struggle for freedom. A properly set trap would have drowned the mink quickly.

Dedicated hunters, on bagging a woodcock, ruffed grouse, or other game bird, will immediately smooth its feathers and, after admiring it briefly, carefully wrap it in newspaper before putting it in the game pocket to carry home in all its pristine beauty. I know the detailed pattern and coloration of feathering of the game birds I have been privileged to take much better than that of the songbirds I have been watching for more than sixty years. The bobwhite quail covey call at dusk or the whistle of woodcock wings in an October aspen thicket are much more esthetic than many birdsongs. Hunting at its best is truly a matter of pure esthetics, surely an affair of the heart.

On Thanksgiving Day in a rural past, few families ever had turkey on the dinner table. A few might serve goose or duck, but chicken was most commonly served. For hunting families, wild game was the dish. The Thanksgiving Day hunt was a tradition for most farm men and boys; it was a long one, starting after chores and a good breakfast and ending in midafternoon. There was no flocking around a radio, and television wasn't known yet. The hunt was long and thorough whatever the weather, making Thanksgiving appetites well earned.

Once back in the farmhouse with the game, the final preparations for the ritual dinner were made. Women bustled to and from the autumn cellar, bringing back armfuls of the season's bounty: cabbages and turnips and parsnips, crocks of new sauerkraut, smoked hams and flitches of bacon to accompany the wild game. For anyone who has ever known a well-stocked cellar, the shelves laden with stored food represent the essence of the provider instinct. Nowadays, economics and ecological consciousness are helping to revive this valued custom of self-sufficiency.

Days grow short in November, as we are reminded in the popular song: There is no time to "play the waiting game." Now is the time to store memories against a less provident future. Some of our finest dreams had their origin in Indian Summers of the past. A thoughtful search for identity during November may provide us with our second chance.

Fittingly, as November starts to fade, we celebrate Thanksgiving. The harvest of the farm is complete; the wild harvest is almost over for the season. Thus, Thanksgiving should be doubly joyful because of the observance of the ancient and the modern harvest together. It pleasantly blends both work and rest, past and present—a fitting way to end the Moon of Michabo.

December

Winter is the most theatrical time of the year. All seasons possess drama, but in this, the most severe season, the elements are the most vigorous and given to swings of wide, dangerous extremes. These dramatic struggles of the weather forces bring stark tragedy and striking beauty, with responsive swings in the spirits of the watchers. There can be terrifying, blinding blizzards with keening winds, followed by the crackling silence of cold, still nights. To the Leni Lenape, December was the Moon When Cold Makes Trees Crack. To the Iroquois, it was the Big Winter Moon; the Northern Cheyennes called it the Big Hard Face Moon. All of these names reflect the Indians' dread of the cold and of the suffering it might bring.

December is a time of skeletal trees, of barren, gray woods filled with dead leaf banks. The cold, cleansing wind purges soil and vegetation, eventually renewing them. All is being prepared for another season of replenishment. Wildlife finds little protection during the Hard Face Moon, and the attrition of the weak begins. The start of winter begins nature's test of the wild creatures and of the environment we provide for them. It emphasizes the importance of wetlands to wildlife, for marshes and swamps are the wintering places for many wildlife species; they provide the best habitat for survival in the cold. The widespread destruction of wetlands is one of the great causes of declining wildlife populations.

December could appropriately be known as the Evergreen Month. Evergreens are a hopeful, dominant element in the wooded winter landscape. The survival of their vegetation through the worst part of the season was recognized by ancient man, and this accounted for its use in earliest solstitial celebrations.

There might be another reason for the favorable attitude toward evergreens. In an insecure past when man was more at the mercy of nature, evergreens provided shelter against the extremes of weather: they protected against cold, boreal winds, and in the heat of summer, they are cool and damp. Thus it would have been easy to associate them with comfort and protection as well as the hope that life would outlast the dark and cold.

There is another sign of hope to be found at this time. The earthstar fungus appears in woodlands; its six- or eight-pointed star base supports a sphere that the imaginative interprets as the earth resting on a star, a benevolent sign of assurance for our world.

By December, it is a Time of Flown Birds, a wistful reference to one of the Cree moons. The remaining birds are puffed out against the cold. While the feathered population is low after migration, some northern birds move down to spend the winter; tinkling junco and tree sparrow songs brighten the day.

With fewer bird species present, feeding stations are especially rewarding. Many persons maintain window feeders. What is needed are more feeding sites in wild, remote areas far from window and yard; there the larger and more shy wildlife species will gather. But make certain they are located in areas of protective cover, for wintering hawks and resident owls scan regularly seeking prey. Europeans have a pleasant, useful custom of preparing an outdoor Christmas tree for the birds; it is decorated with various kinds of bird food.

December is a month of numerous clear, sharp images involving birds. It is a time when Currier and Ives scenes may be observed by those with discerning eyes, scenes that will linger in the mind. A ruffed grouse steps carefully across a snowy sandstone elevation; its tracks show the snowshoes the species grows every winter. It pauses to feed on partridgeberries or wintergreen berries in the cold, red sunset rays, then flies to a thick hemlock roost for the night. A set of ring-necked pheasant tracks lead into a winter swamp, through buttonbush thickets and bushy swamp-grass tangles. They pause under a bright-berried swamp holly bush, then trail on through the swamp to a gravel-knolled cornfield. The bird feeds on fallen corn, then returns to the swamp to spend the night in a sheltered patch of swamp grass. A short-eared owl, perched on a high muskrat house, watches the wandering pheasant with unblinking eyes. Dark open water in a partially frozen lake is host to wintering waterfowl, mostly black ducks and mallards with a scattering of bluebills and a pair of whistlers. They command attention with their distinctive antics performed against a frigid, wintry landscape. A cluster of ever-greens harbors northern migrants and perhaps a saw-whet owl. A lonely country road through a snowy waste is alive with horned larks and perhaps some longspurs seeking gravel.

With the start of severe weather, wildlife drifts to the low-lands where the best cover remains. That is where experienced outdoorsmen go to seek it—bird student or hunter. Following the track of a fox on such a trip, I saw where it had killed a shrew, then a short distance away, it had dropped the little mammal. Seton writes that foxes will kill shrews and moles, then drop or bury them while they hunt for more palatable prey; if they find nothing better, they will return to consume the discarded item.

Sumac or wild apple trees near good cover will be gnawed when severe weather and food scarcity forces rabbits to feed on bark. White-tailed bucks, now wearing their gray winter coats, start dropping their antlers late in December. And if cold and snow have persisted long enough, tracks of hungry coons will be found. Small mammal sign is noticeable; their runways lace the vegetative cover. Their tracks, tunnels, and holes are usually the most visible sign of life in the snow.

Snow may be inconvenient, but to outdoorsmen it offers the greatest opportunity to study wildlife habits, especially the earth-bound mammals. Reading the "newsprint" pressed in the snow by the night writers brings the observer up-to-date on the activities of winter wildlife, as the snow carries a complete, unedited record of the night's struggles. It also gives accurate information on the population of various species to the tracker skilled in reading and interpreting tracks and other sign. Wildlife tracks in new snow reveal original, distinctive patterns; they express the individuality of each animal as well as the species.

My elderly Ashtabula County friend, one of the finest woodsmen I ever knew, taught me much about tracking. Following the trail of a fox, he knew its sex; furthermore, he could determine the direction of the wind when the animal was hunting by its approach to cover, its age from the caution it exhibited, and the onset of mating season from the pattern of its tracks. To this outdoorsman, it was all a case of straight-line logic.

Hunting rabbits when there is a good tracking snow is one of the fine winter pastimes. In times past, rabbit hunts during the Christmas holidays were eagerly anticipated. A group of boys would hunt the neighborhood, tramping out all the good cover patches. And often game would appear on the Christmas dinner table.

The winter solstice has been a test of human faith for centuries. Men of ancient times always dreaded the cold, dark time of the shortest days of the year and attempted to counter this fear by bringing into their homes all the elements of nature which had brought them comfort and joy through the year. Evergreens, which thrive through the winter, brought them hope that they too might survive the difficult period, and they sought that reassurance in a living symbol of the tree. They decorated their homes with evergreen branches, weaving them into unending wreaths, adding to the hope for eternity. So much importance was attached to evergreens from those early times that we have never lost that close association with them.

The hearth with its bright, warm blaze was the center of their lives throughout winter. They brightened their evergreen decorations with tinsel probably suggested by dew-laden spider webs, icicles, and snow. Mistletoe, used by the Druids in ancient solstial rites, was added to the decoration; it was so revered for its mysterious powers that its gathering and use were governed by strict, ritualistic rules. Early hunters wore a sprig of mistletoe in their hats to assure good hunting.

The pull of the hearth is stronger in December as the need for heat and light grows—the treasures of the cold, dark months. The Scandinavians originated the tradition of the Yule log. During its burning through the long nights of solstice, old hatreds also went up the chimney. The ancient Germans added their own invention; during the log's burning, they invited the presence of Bertha, goddess of the hearth and domesticity, into their homes for the coming year to foster a happy homelife, and to shelter them from fear, superstition, and a harsh, threatening world.

The name *Bertha* means the bright, luminous one of special understanding; her proper night came at the end of the twelve days of Christmas, later to become Epiphany.

With the advent of Christianity, many of the pagan rites were adapted to the new religion, and modern Christianity represents a blend of the best of pagan and Christian customs. Even today, Christmas represents hope and reassurance largely in the form of the ancient symbols. Martin Luther is credited with having the first Christmas tree, a fir. The evergreen as a Christmas tree is the tree of life, proof that life outlasts darkness, coldness, and human despair. Fir, spruce, pine, and even hemlock and cedar have served as Christmas trees, and holly and mistletoe still brighten homes. Modern decorators are using more and more outdoor products in holiday decorating; cones, pods, burrs, nuts, acorns, and other native products appear. I once saw a small wreath made of lycopodium, swamp holly, and bittersweet—a most original decoration—offered for sale by two impoverished children.

Despite the need for brightness and cheer, Christmas was an austere day of prayer and fasting for many years in early America due to the beliefs of the Puritans. The influence of German and southern customs gradually changed the holiday until it became the bright, joyful holy day we know today. Thus, from the cold, dark time of hopelessness and fear has developed the brightest period of the year for modern man. Yet even though holiday merriment abounds, it should not be overlooked that the human spirit still needs an occasional boost. The customs of pagans and moderns grew out of this need, and through the centuries, indomitable, unselfish individuals have sought to brighten the gloomier moments. These individuals who bring hope and cheer to others when they are most needed are the spirits who have given meaning to existence through the centuries. It is they who have brought significance to life, and custom and legend to our heritage. We owe them much!

Memories of Christmas past come back to create a pleasant glow. There was the community skating party—images of the creek filled with young and old familiar figures, leisurely skating between the big bonfires located at each end of a quarter-mile stretch of safe, smooth ice, making the world seem safe and pleasant. I recall the sight of a lone farm boy running a trapline to earn money for the Christmas season, or perhaps the image is one of the entire school body gathered at a bridge, skating or sliding on the ice, or watching a vigorous game of duck-on-the-rock. The balletic efforts of the players leaping to escape the huge clubs thundering over the ice toward the "duck" in its circle remains one of the humorous images of our vigorous rural-school recreation. Sledding parties and games of "fox and geese" were less brutal activities, but all of them bring to mind a distant, more quiet way of life.

Now, near the end of the calendar year, I am doubly appreciative that I changed from a rigid scientific approach to the outdoors. This change toward subjectivity has brought peace and happiness. I read that Edvard Grieg, the Norwegian composer, began studying the highly personal folk music of his country, and the effort made a great change in his life. "I learned to know my own nature," he wrote. When I made the change from a cold, scientific approach to the highly personal, subjective approach, I eventually learned to know my own true nature. I confirmed that the senses are more reliable than cold, calculating thought; they permit one to find his or her own original view, the only truth for the individual and one not prescribed by rule.

On luminous snowy moonlight nights when shadows are dark and deep in contrast to the brightly lighted fields, a restless spell falls on the observer. I recall taking a long walk on such a night with my elderly friend in Ashtabula County. There was a December snow on the ground, and the temperature was so low that the snow "zeeped" underfoot with every step. Our destination was the wide, wild, swampy bottomland near his home, an area he knew like the back of his hand. Tracks were abundant along the way, especially rabbit tracks, and occasionally we would glimpse a rabbit frolicking in the snow, equally as captive to the bright, white night as were we.

At the edge of the swamp, my friend brushed the snow from a log and we sat down, a large sugar tree to our backs. "Now, I'll show you how to call in a hoot owl," he said. He gave a three-syllabled hoot of the great horned owl. Almost immediately there was an answer from the woods, for the owls were beginning to defend nesting territory. By giving a low call at proper intervals, Charlie tolled the owl toward us. Suddenly the big bird silently flew in and lit in a nearby tree. Then it uttered its haunting call. The sound, though surprisingly low and soft at such close range, was made with great force, giving it carrying quality. The owl flew on after an unanswered interval; it was too close for another hoot. The old outdoorsman called it in once more. Again we witnessed the silent flight of the great form in the moonlight and heard close at hand this modern voice of the wilderness.

We sat for a long time listening to owl calls and watching the heavens and the broad valley slopes. Polaris marked the northern sky, which had been cleared by the strong breath of Boreas. Beyond the swampy lowlands, orderly field outlines were plainly visible in the night light. Man and nature appeared to be in ecologic balance in this peaceful setting. We experienced a great sense of contentment.

MOODS OF THE OHIO MOONS

was composed in 10½/12 Aldus
on a Xyvision system with Linotron 202 output
by BookMasters, Inc.;
printed by sheet-fed offset
on 55-pound Glatfelter B-31 acid-free stock,
Smyth sewn and bound over .088″ binders' boards
in Holliston Kingston Natural cloth,
with 80-pound Rainbow Antique endpapers,
and wrapped in dust jackets printed in two colors
on 80-pound enamel stock and film laminated;
also adhesive bound with paper covers printed in two colors
on 10-point coated-one-side stock and film laminated;
by Cushing-Malloy, Inc.;
designed by Will Underwood;
and published by

THE KENT STATE UNIVERSITY PRESS
Kent, Ohio 44242